HAUNTED UNIVERSAL STUDIOS

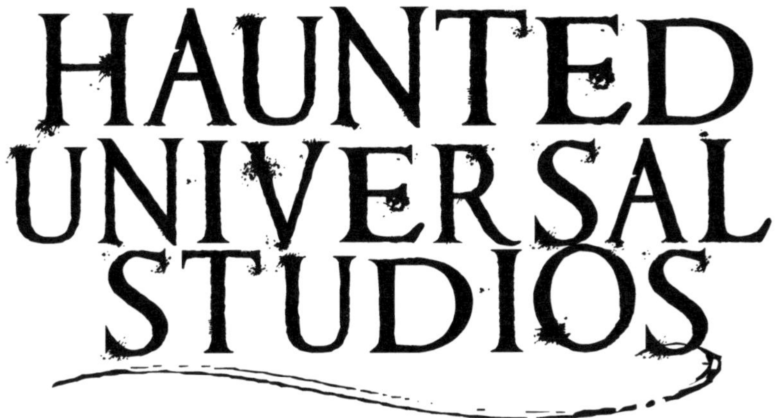

BRIAN CLUNE WITH BOB DAVIS

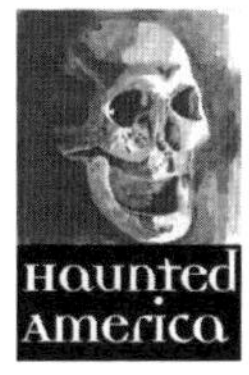

Published by Haunted America
A Division of The History Press
Charleston, SC
www.historypress.net

All photos in this book are from the authors' private collection.

First published 2018

Manufactured in the United States

ISBN 9781467141215

Library of Congress Control Number: 2018943600

Notice: The information in this book is true and complete to the best of our knowledge. It is offered without guarantee on the part of the authors or The History Press. The authors and The History Press disclaim all liability in connection with the use of this book.

This book is dedicated to the memory of Ash Blackwell and Gerald Reynolds. Their friendship and kindness has spread magic that will last forever to those of us who were blessed with knowing them!

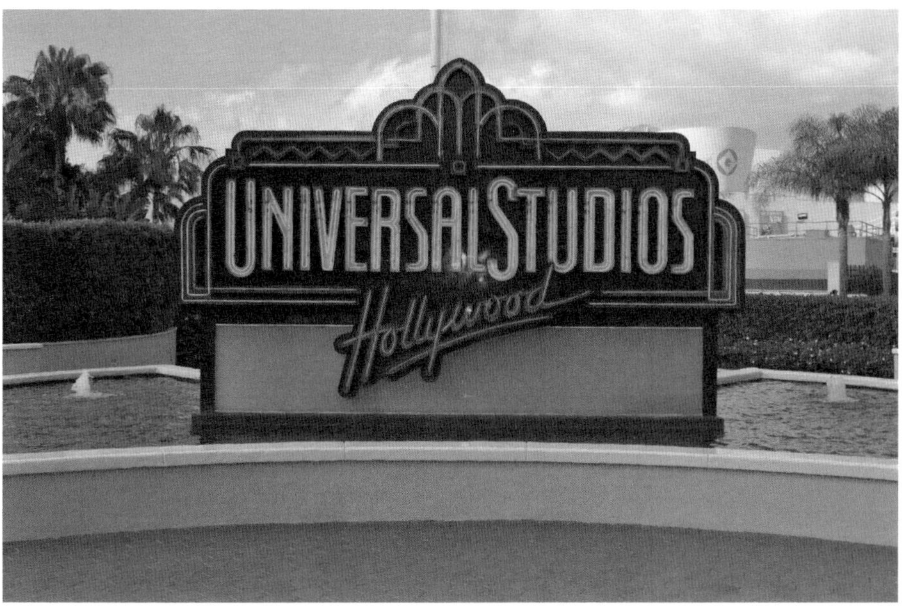

The sign at the entrance to the park welcomes visitors.

CONTENTS

FOREWORD

Brilliant! Absolutely brilliant!

Universal Studios Hollywood is a magical world of adventure, imagination and art that comes alive as entertainment. However, what is obscured behind the curtain of storytelling may be a hidden past filled with earthly hauntings we have yet to uncover or understand.

With that being said, as I read eagerly from page to page, I recalled one of my very first ghostly experiences. Bear with me as I share a story that I haven't shared with many. The events you are about to read would become the reason that I delved wholeheartedly into paranormal research.

I had the wonderful pleasure of working for Universal Studios Hollywood from 1999 through 2009. I had the opportunity of working various locations throughout the theme park, and I was able to experience and learn the trade quite quickly. I originally worked the Terminator 2: 3D show and was able to witness Arnold Schwarzenegger fly in on a helicopter for the action-packed grand opening. Wow! Looking in awe at the crowd, I was amazed. I would love to be part of making so many people happy. It was the following year, 2000, that I had the opportunity to audition for the part of the Deacon in the Water World show; I had become a stuntman and had been working on many films. I was really enjoying my work, and when I wasn't scheduled to play the Deacon in Water World, I had the chance to cross-train at other rides within the park. That same year, I was training at the Back to the Future ride—now known as The Simpsons ride.

The training took place during the non-peak season, so there were not too many guests at the park during this time. I was positioned in an area where I supervised the guests dividing into separate lines, which would guide them down a curved hallway. At the end of the hallway, they would be assisted by another Universal employee in boarding the cars. Due to the curve in the hallway, there is a camera positioned to assist me in watching the guests as they make their way safely to the next employee. A young couple came in, and I sent them to my right, which led to another Universal employee who then directed the guests into the pre-ride room to watch a short video before boarding the ride.

About fifteen seconds after the couple passed, a young blond-haired girl, approximately nine years old, came running past me; she ran down the right-side hallway where I had just sent the young couple. At that time, I looked at the camera display screen and watched the young girl running down the curved hallway to ensure that she reached my co-worker safely. On the display, I saw the young girl run directly past my co-worker and into the pre-ride room the young couple had just entered. I didn't even have a chance to notify my co-worker, but I did see her enter the pre-ride room. After a few minutes, the ride was over. I saw the young couple leave the room, and they both headed toward the exit. I waited, watching for the young blond girl to exit the room, but she did not come out.

I walked down the hall toward the pre-ride room and asked my co-worker, "Where is the little girl?"

"What little girl?" he replied.

"The little girl that ran right past you into the room with the couple."

He told me that there was no little girl, and he didn't see one on the ride or anywhere near the hallway. The question he asked me then will forever haunt me. "You saw her, didn't you? You saw the little girl?" he asked.

I was in shock to think I had just seen the ghost of a young child, not only with my own eyes but also through the camera display screen.

My co-worker went on to tell me that the little girl had been there for a few years and that several employees, along with the maintenance repair crew and the night cleaning crew, had heard a little girl giggling. I was also told that some of the women from the night cleaning crew refused to work in the building. It was at that time I wondered who this little blond-haired spirit could possibly be. I learned that there had been a young female child who had a pre-existing brain aneurysm that ruptured while she was on the ride. I have come to believe this is the spirit that roams the entire park.

I was allowed to do an after-hours investigation, but it was during my interviews with other park employees that I learned many of them have seen a blond child of about nine years old. If they haven't seen her, they certainly have heard her giggling throughout several locations of the park.

By the year 2004, I was well into paranormal investigating and the claims at Universal seemed to keep me busy. However, on May 21, 2004, the Revenge of the Mummy ride, located down in the lower lot, was opened to the public. Not long after the ride opened, I began getting reports from the Mummy ride employees, as well as security guards and park supervisors, indicating that guests were frantic, scared and worried about what they were seeing on the tracks of the ride.

The reports indicated that the witnesses were seeing a young boy. He was described as having black hair, his age ranged from eight to twelve years old and he was wearing old-fashioned clothing. Due to the fact that nobody knew who the boy was or where the boy had come from, the ride was shut down in order to search for him, but he was never found.

This was not a onetime account. Reports began coming in almost daily and lasted for a few months. Some of the park employees said that they had seen the boy at the Ben and Jerry's Ice Cream store located next door to the Mummy ride. Unfortunately, by the time I was available to investigate these claims, the sightings had ended.

I met Brian Clune and Bob Davis, owners of Planet Paranormal, in 2007, during a paranormal convention aboard the *Queen Mary* in Long Beach, California. I have had the honor of investigating with them both on multiple occasions, and I still utilize the research and investigational techniques they have shared with me.

Haunted Universal Studios is one of the most captivating haunts that I have read in a long time. Brian Clune and Bob Davis have done amazing, and extensive, historical research in order to bring you some of the best-kept secrets of Universal Studios Hollywood.

—Syd Schultz II
Director of Paranormal Bootcamp Events

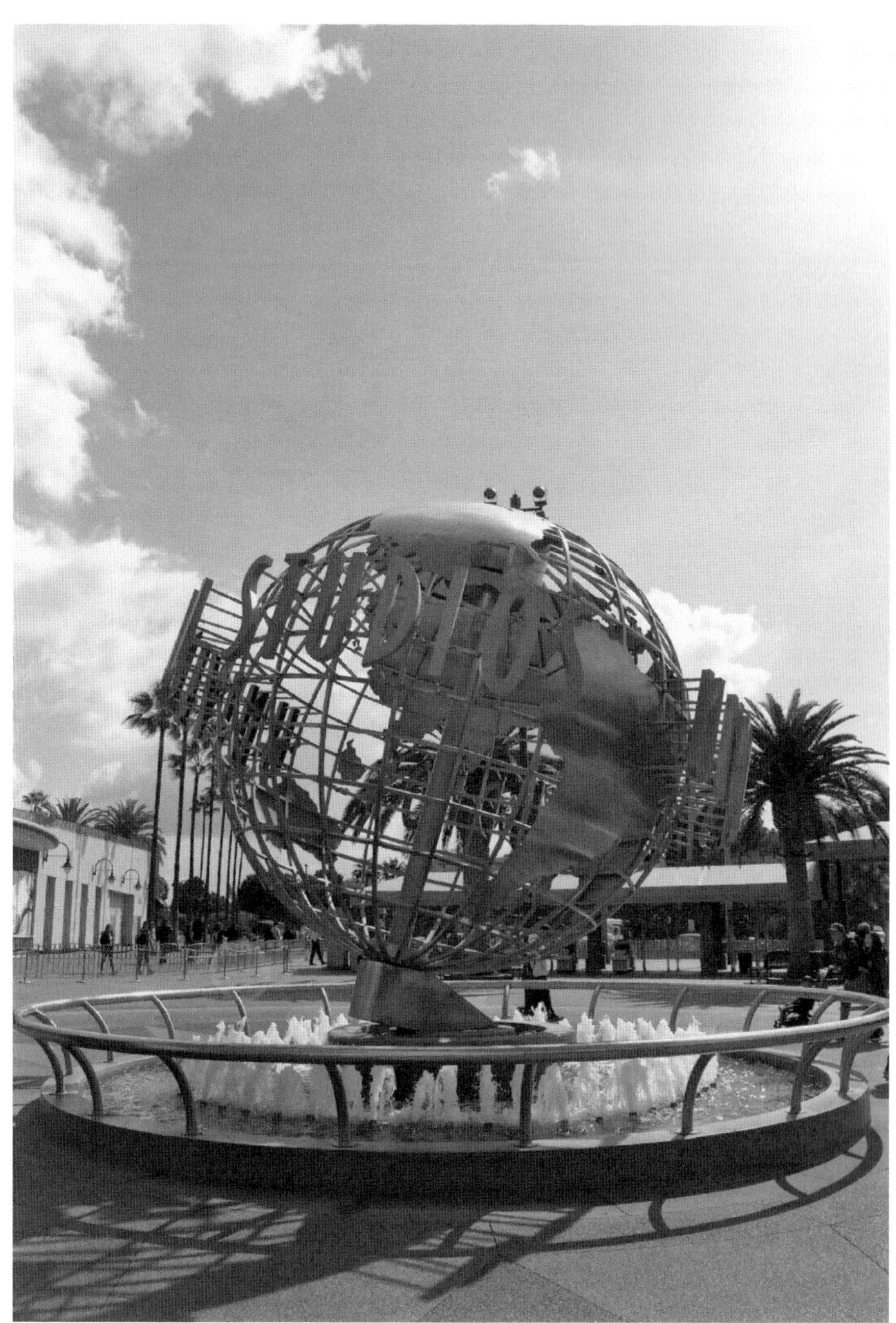

Universal Studios sculpture.

ACKNOWLEDGEMENTS

We would like to thank The History Press once more for allowing us to write for them. Our new acquisitions editor, Laurie Krill, had to field our many questions, complaints and prattling and did so with the utmost professionalism, friendship and cheer. Thank you, Laurie. We would like to thank the many employees of Universal Studios and CityWalk who spoke with us and told us many of the tales within the book. We would also like to thank all of those within the paranormal community for trusting us to write books they enjoy and the loyalty they have shown by egging us on to write even more tales for them—chief among these Corrine Cortez, our biggest fan. As always, we must thank our families. Without them, we wouldn't be able to do what we do. Special thanks to Terri Clune for being the best spell-check and initial editor an author can have. Thank you, everyone!

INTRODUCTION
A HOLLYWOOD LEGACY

I think cinema, movies, and magic have always been closely associated. The very earliest people who made film were magicians.
—Francis Ford Coppola

Hollywood has always been known as a land where dreams come true. It is also known as a place where nightmares lurk in the shadows cast by the klieg lights. Many aspiring actors and actresses come to Hollywood seeking both fame and fortune; most find only heartache and disappointment. For those strong enough to come to grips with their dreams of stardom being dashed on the Hollywood Walk of Fame, they limp home to a common life of work and hopefully a comfortable retirement. For those not strong enough, life becomes one big regret from which they can never recover. Some turn to a life of drugs or alcohol in an attempt to forget their failure, while others seek a permanent solution to their despair. One such person has become the stuff of legend, not for the way she lived her life but rather the way she ended it.

Peg Entwistle was an up-and-coming actress from Great Britain who was beginning to shine on Broadway. Like so many others in the early days of Hollywood, Peg thought that she could make it big in Tinseltown. Once she moved out to California, she struggled to get roles until she was finally cast in her first big Hollywood production. Unfortunately, her scene was cut from the David O. Selznick film *Thirteen Women*, and that was the final straw for the distraught Entwistle. On September 16, 1932, drunk and grief-stricken,

Peg Entwistle climbed up to the top of the H of the Hollywoodland sign and jumped the forty-five feet to her death. Peg has been haunting the sign ever since. Unfortunately, Peg Entwistle's is not the only spirit that has become famous over time in this city of make believe; on the contrary, Hollywood is considered by many people to be the most haunted city in the United States.

It is a well-accepted theory in the research into paranormal activity that strong emotions at the time of death can be a catalyst for spirits to remain behind. Love and hate are two of the strongest emotions that a human being can feel, and these emotions are probably the two most common found in Hollywood. Look at all of the stories that have come out of this town: love affairs abound, marriages broken up almost daily due to infidelity, and many of these lead to deeds too horrible to mention. Some of these unmentionables have taken place at the various studios dotting the landscape. Then there are those whose love of their craft is so deep that they can't let it go even in death. These individuals care so deeply for not only their artistry but also the studios themselves that their spirits remain behind to watch over a place they loved in life.

Fear is another emotion that brings out strong psychic waves from a person. What goes through people's minds at the moment they realize that they could die, that the rail they thought would hold them up in the catwalk has failed and they are falling, possibly to their death? Working a movie set on or off a sound stage is a dangerous endeavor. Overhead lights, sandbags and weights, screens and filters, ladders and steps all play a part in a possible accident, some deadly. This has become a known quantity among stagehands and grips, a way of life that must be acknowledged yet put at the back of one's mind. Never let it be said that some of these stage workers have less of a love for their craft than those in front of the camera. Many of these behind-the-scenes heroes are just as dedicated, if not more so than the actors they help to make look good on screen. Many have refused to leave even after death has claimed them.

With all of the sad and sometimes horrendous deaths that have taken place in Hollywood can one really fail to see why it is sometimes called the most haunted city? Universal Studios is one of the oldest studios in Hollywood and the largest studio ever built—after all, it is called Universal City. With the vast amount of public access that has been granted even before the studio became a themed entertainment park, is it any wonder that it would also be one of the most haunted studios in Hollywood?

Many tales abound in the studio's various lots, some stemming from the very beginning, others as new as day. For those expecting gruesome and

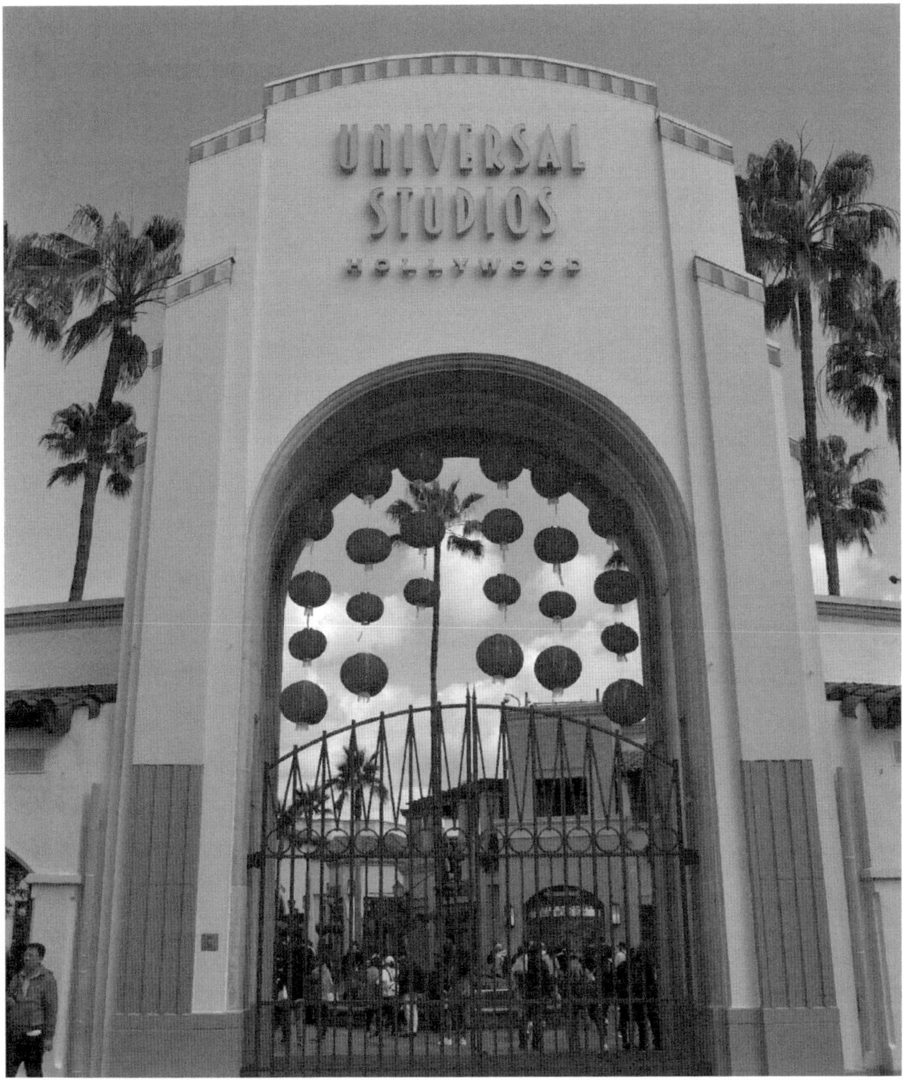

The arches guests pass under to enter into the studio have now become synonymous with the theme park around the world.

horrific tales, be warned, most of the spirits at Universal are more helpful than horrible. Some are secretive and private, others just want to be remembered and others go about their craft as if they are still in the full of life. One thing is for certain: Universal Studios is most assuredly one of the most haunted locations in all of Hollywoodland.

1
The Man behind the Magic

Today, Universal Studios is mainly known as an amusement park, a place to go for thrills and chills and where fans can see their favorite TV and movie characters come to life or visit Hogwarts and the world of Harry Potter. Even while guests are relaxing on the back-lot tram tour and casting their gazes on movie sets from Hollywood's historic past, they still seem almost oblivious to the fact that Universal is a working, functional movie studio. Universal put the horror movie genre on the map and stopped one of America's greatest inventors from holding a monopoly on film production that would have changed the way we all view movies today. Universal Studios' history cannot be fully understood without knowing who had the dream to make Hollywood what it is today, and who it was that had the strength and determination to fight, and win, against a corporate giant to make Tinseltown the glamor capital of the world.

Carl Laemmle was born in 1867 in the Jewish area near Laupheim, Germany. His father was a cattle merchant and part-time land trader, but the family still struggled financially. Carl and his siblings grew up in poverty. He was one of the youngest of eleven children; however, only three other siblings survived into adulthood, the others having passed due to sickness and epidemic. By the age of thirteen, Carl had gotten a job as an apprentice and was supporting his family while continuing his education. During his time as an apprentice, Laemmle learned the art of salesmanship and accounting, lessons he would put to good use later in life.

By the time Carl was seventeen years old, he was ready to leave his old life behind. After his mother passed away and after reading all of the letters his brother Joseph had been sending from America, Carl decided to join him in the United States. Carl's father gave him his blessing, fifty dollars and two tickets on the SS *Necker*, one for Carl and one for Carl's longtime friend Leo Hirschfeld. Carl had failed to inform his brother that he would be arriving in New York; there was no one to meet him at the docks, so the two men were taken to a boardinghouse by one of the relatives of travel companions they had met on the voyage from Europe. After about two weeks of doing odd jobs around New York City, Carl began looking for his brother and found him working in Chicago, Illinois, as a secretary to the vice-president of a German-language newspaper. Joseph sent his brother ten dollars and a bus ticket to Chicago, and Carl was on his way to the Windy City.

Once in Chicago, Carl made a meager living doing odd jobs all over the city; he even tried his hand at farming in South Dakota for a short time but found that he had no desire or talent for that type of work. Carl did say, however, that his time at the farm taught him the value of a dollar more than any job he ever had; he also said it was the hardest job he ever worked. After only seven weeks of life on the farm, Carl Laemmle found himself back in Chicago, working low-paying, dead-end jobs and depending on his brother's charity to get by in life. Even though his life in America was not turning out the way Carl had planned, after several trips back to his hometown in Germany, Laemmle knew that life in the United States was what his destiny demanded. He applied for United States citizenship and took the oath of loyalty in 1889, and America became his home.

In 1894, Laemmle moved to Oshkosh, Wisconsin, to begin working as the bookkeeper of the Continental Clothing Company. It had been ten years since Laemmle had arrived in America, and Carl had finally found a job that not only paid well but allowed him to pursue creative avenues as well. Laemmle had always been intrigued by showmanship and now decided to learn the ins and outs of publicity and the ways in which flamboyance played a key part. Laemmle began creating and distributing catalogues that were artistic and catered to customers. He began to upgrade the mediocre advertising of the company with bold, creative ad campaigns and designed window displays. Through it all, he asked for customer feedback to keep up with trends to keep the company competitive and up-to-date. All of Carl's hard work paid off when Sam Stern promoted him to a management position. Carl was now set in his career at the clothing company. In 1898, Carl married Sam Stern's niece Recha Stern, and together they had two children: Rosabelle and Julius. He was voted "[o]ne of the fifteen most eminent and enterprising businessmen in Oshkosh in 1905." Laemmle had a beautiful family and a career that put him in the high upper class of society, yet he was not content.

In 1906, Carl Laemmle decided to go into business for himself. He had amassed savings of just over $3,000 (roughly $75,000 today) and planned on investing that money in a chain of retail stores catering to low- and middle-income customers. While scouting the city of Chicago for a good location to open up his first store, he noticed a long line of people standing outside one of the new nickelodeons. Intrigued by the growing crowd, Laemmle waited in the line and, once inside, became enthralled by what he saw and the way the people reacted to the moving pictures. Laemmle knew that this was the wave of the future, that people would flock to the picture shows and hand over their hard-earned money to get away from the daily rigors and worries of life. He decided right then and there that this was what he would put his savings into, this was the business he would invest his future in.

Laemmle observed the nickelodeon he had found along with others in the city and was amazed at the constant flow of people handing over ten cents to enter the storefront theater. Most businesspeople believed that the moving pictures were simply a trend, a flash-in-the-pan amusement that would die out in short time and be gone; after all, how many people would actually stay amused sitting in a dark theater, watching pictures flit across a small screen while music played in time to the scene? Most thought moving pictures had about five years before the stage regained its prominence and the movie houses went the way of the dodo. After watching the crowds endlessly handing over their money, Carl Laemmle was one of the few who knew motion pictures were here to stay. Laemmle took his savings and opened his first nickelodeon, the White Front Theater, on Chicago's Milwaukee Avenue. This first theater was so successful that it didn't take long before Carl was able to open a second venue, the Family Theater, which also did extremely well. By all accounts, Laemmle was on his way to a prosperous business venture. Carl, however, saw another way to expand his fortunes. One of the things that Laemmle noticed with his theaters was the hassle in renting the films he was showing. The nickelodeons had a high-volume turnaround of films, needing to change daily, sometimes twice a day, so it became frustrating having to deal with the various studios' distribution divisions, each trying to get its movies and shorts into the movie houses that would show them and each making the theater owners buy the films at high prices but also making them wait on the reels to actually show up. Film exchanges solved the problem of having to buy the films, and many theater owners were happy to rent. The exchanges were still slow to arrive at the venues, if they arrived at all, and many of the films would be withdrawn for payment issues before the theater owner could get them spooled up. Laemmle became so frustrated with trying to get films for his theaters that he decided to start up his own exchange—run his way—with higher efficiency than the exchanges he would compete with.

Laemmle knew the importance of being independent and that other noncorporate theater owners felt the same way, so when Carl opened up his Laemmle Film Service, he was determined to make it easier and cheaper for the independent theater owners to obtain the films they needed to make a profit. Laemmle became so successful with his exchange that by 1908, he had opened offices in Chicago and six other states from the West Coast to the Great Lakes. In just two years, Laemmle had become the largest film distributer in America. Laemmle, never one to shy away from notoriety, wanted his exchange to be known not only for its quality of service but for its name recognition as well. One of the things that had always been important in Carl Laemmle's life was for a man to live up to his word, so when Laemmle told a customer that the film he was renting for his theater would arrive on such a date and at such a cost, Laemmle made sure that it would be in his customer's hand when it was supposed to be. This dedication to customer service earned him the respect of everyone he dealt with. There were those, however, who were watching what Carl was doing and who were not happy that he was taking business away from them.

Standing at just five feet, three inches, Carl Laemmle was not what one would call an imposing figure—what he lacked in stature he made up in pure determination and tenacity. It may have been Laemmle's decided lack of height that caused one of the most respected inventors and scientists in the history of the United States and the world to mistake size for ability and brains, leading to one of Thomas Alva Edison's worst defeats. Edison had invented the Kinetoscope in 1888 and soon improved this early movie camera to the point where movies became a successful entertainment industry. Edison not only produced and sold his cameras through his company, the Edison Manufacturing Company, but he also began to produce motion pictures for mass audiences. By 1894, as a way to protect his fledgling motion picture business, Edison had gathered together a legal team to harass and bring lawsuits against other companies involved in motion picture production for infringement. Edison, using scare tactics and the threat of lawsuits, managed to put many of his competitors out of business or forced them to pay monthly licensing fees for the use of cameras that they had already purchased from him. By 1909, Edison had coerced his main competitor, the Biograph Company, along with Eastman Kodak, which provided the film for his movie cameras, to join into a conglomerate. Together they formed the Motion Picture Patents Company, also known as the Edison Trust. Now combined with the most powerful and influential film companies, Edison was able to establish a monopoly on cameras, projectors and film and allowed his trust to impose a monthly two-dollar tax on all film production companies, producers and exchange owners who used any of his, Kodak's or Biograph's inventions, which was everyone at the time. Laemmle, at the helm of the largest exchange company in the country, was naturally upset at the added cost of doing business and considered Edison's tax not only illegal but a monopoly as well. Laemmle decided to fight back, and Edison responded with over three hundred lawsuits spread out over the lifetime of the battle between the two stubborn men.

Carl Laemmle was an intelligent man and realized from the very beginning that he would be unable to take on Edison and his trust by himself. Laemmle knew that there were many independent film producers and studios who were not at all happy with the situation they found themselves in, and he not only organized these independents into a cohesive unit but also became their de facto leader. Laemmle accomplished this feat by becoming one of them, by forming his own production company, the Independent Moving Picture Company (IMP). After creating his new company and organizing the other independents to fight against Edison, Laemmle tried his case in the highest court in the land, the court of public opinion. As the public slowly came over to his side, he again employed a new and powerful weapon in the fight. Knowing that the public liked their idols, Laemmle instituted something that had been not only forbidden in the field of moviemaking but feared as well. Laemmle knew that it would be the final piece in the puzzle of defeating Edison and his stranglehold over the equipment needed to make moviemaking the business he knew it could become. This new weapon became known as the "star system."

During the early days of the nickelodeon and silent film era, the stars were treated as nothing more than simple commodities. The reason for this attitude had to do with the fear of actors becoming too big in the eyes of the moviegoing public. Stars who were idolized and in demand would be able to demand more perks, more concessions and, worst of all, more pay for their rolls—this is why the actors and actresses of the early cinema were not known by their names but by titles such as Baby-face, Little Mary or the Girl with Curls. Edison and the other members of his trust knew this and were appalled when they found out that Laemmle had begun putting the stars' names out to the public and promoting and advertising them. Edison couldn't understand how Laemmle could be so inept at business as to undermine his own profits in this way but figured that in the long run, this would do the job of eliminating the troublesome Laemmle for them. Laemmle, for his part, knew that this idea would cost him money up front but could, in the long run, garner him more profits from the star power he was creating. Laemmle began offering more money to trust actors than Edison was willing to pay and placing actors under contract with IMP. In this way, Laemmle managed to "create" the careers of notables like King Baggot and Mary Pickford. The advertising ploy worked to perfection, and IMP began to grow along with its profits. In 1915, the Supreme Court ruled that the Edison Trust was in violation of the Sherman Antitrust laws for "hampering free competition in the creation of a monopoly," and the Motion Pictures Parents Company, after having sued Carl Laemmle 289 times, was ordered dissolved. Carl Laemmle and the independents had won against a seemingly unstoppable, wealthy and powerful group of America's premier business icons. This victory was only the beginning for the man who was about to usher in the magic of moviemaking and bring dreams to the silver screen.

2

The Magic Moves to Hollywood

Three years before the Edison Trust was ordered to dissolve, Carl Laemmle and his group of investors and film producers created the Universal Film Manufacturing Company and moved all of their production facilities from Chicago to Fort Lee, New Jersey. Once the issues with Edison and his trust had been settled and all of his attention could be focused on making films, Laemmle knew that if he was going to continue to grow his company, he would need to expand his operations. Laemmle had invested some of his money in a ramshackle studio in Hollywood, California, at the corner of Gower and Sunset Boulevards, and by 1911, he had begun making films on the West Coast. His main studio was still in Fort Lee, but as production grew out in sunny Southern California, Laemmle began to realize the inherent advantages of the almost perpetual sunshine on the cost of producing films. This realization led Laemmle to seek out a larger lot where he could expand his West Coast production facilities and, in so doing, his profits as well. In August 1912, the Universal Film Manufacturing Company leased the Oak Crest Ranch in the San Fernando Valley and began transforming it into a bona fide film lot.

Once the lease was in place, Laemmle built a series of stages and outdoor movie sets, including a Native American village replete with Chimallo actors and actresses and one hundred horses from the Isleta Reservation near Albuquerque, New Mexico, and enough housing to accommodate up to sixty-five families, who would become permanent residents living on the studio grounds. The first official opening of the new Universal Oak Crest

Ranch was held on December 10, 1912, and the event was open to the public. Invitations were sent out to actors and actresses from the other studios along with hand-delivered invites to state and local politicians and dignitaries. Laemmle was not one to skimp when it came to promoting his interests, and he wanted the opening of his new studio to stand out.

Carl Laemmle was not content with having an ordinary movie studio. He figured that if he was going to make films the way he wanted, he would need to have everything he needed already on hand for use. To this end, Laemmle brought in horses, created workshops where carriages and other props could be built and stored and even had a complete western town built along with other street façades permanently erected on his leased lot. Laemmle once quipped that he had built his own city, and that simple statement gave him an idea. On July, 10, 1913, Universal Oak Crest Ranch had its second grand opening—this time, however, it was to celebrate the changing of its name to that of Universal City. Once again, politicians and the public were invited to marvel at what Laemmle had built in the foothills near Hollywood. The big attraction at this gala event was the Universal City Zoo. The zoo was really nothing more than a small menagerie consisting of a few sheep, goats, horses and one pig, but the crowd seemed enthralled that the studio had its own animals on hand. The zoo itself would grow to house many different types of wildlife, including an elephant, a lion and exotic birds from all around the world.

The success of the two grand openings prompted Laemmle to open his studio to the public on a daily basis. Laemmle had many photographs taken of the sets and stages to promote renting them out to other studios and individual producers, and he figured that with the rental money—along with the small five-cent admission fee charged to the public to see how movies were made—his profits would grow. Part of the appeal for moving to Hollywood was the scenery provided by the Los Angeles River, the Santa Monica Mountains and the nearby desert landscape; these same assets also helped lure the public to Universal City. The crowds loved watching the gunfights in the western towns as the cowboys battled the rampaging Native Americans or the local sheriff squared off in the dusty main street of town—outdrawing the outlaw in a one-on-one duel for law and order and the town damsel in distress. Universal City was a complete success, and things couldn't have been going better for Universal Studios and its investors. Laemmle, however, was not content. He saw the success as a sign that the studio needed to expand and grow. If it was to become the premier studio in Hollywood, it needed more room.

The idea of growing the company was not universally agreed upon by the partners, but eventually, Laemmle gained sole ownership of Universal Film Manufacturing and immediately began looking for a new plot of land. What the company found was a large, 230-acre plot along Lankershim Boulevard, which included the Nestor Ranch, Taylor Ranch and Boag, Davis and Hershey Ranches. Laemmle promptly bought the property for a whopping $165,000. Once the sale was complete, Universal began a wide, sweeping construction project in October 1914 that included six hundred sets, ninety stages, a bank, a post office, living areas, a school for those children living on studio grounds, a new zoo and a police station. Laemmle had actually attained his dream of building his own city.

The new Universal City was built directly across the street from where the Treaty of Guadalupe Hidalgo, which ended the Mexican-American War, was signed. The *Ogden City Standard* described the site as "occupying a comparatively level plateau, forming the front of a basin something over a mile in diameter, entirely surrounded by mountains. From the center of the 'city' one obtains a view of a greater diversity of scenery than is possible in any other place in America." In other words, a perfect place to make movies. Formal groundbreaking took place in May 1914, and production of *Damon and Pythias* began in July of the same year. Laemmle held his third grand opening on October 15, 1914, but this celebration was for employees of the studio and their families only. It was meant to show them how important Laemmle thought they were and how he thought of them as family. It was at this event that he announced the plans for a huge, public opening planned for February 2, 1915. He told those gathered that it would be the grandest spectacle the state had ever seen and would be remembered for generations to come.

As the construction of the new studio progressed, it became clear that it would not be completed in time for the February deadline, and the grand opening was pushed back until March 15. Always the showman, Carl Laemmle not only planned a spectacle for the opening of his new Universal City but he also created a way to prolong the event by planning a train trip from Chicago, Illinois, to Hollywood with whistle stops in Denver, Albuquerque, the Grand Canyon and other sites along the way. He even came up with a name for himself and those he invited to ride along on the trip, "Universalites."

Universal Studio executives, news reporters, exhibitors, invited actors and actresses and a filmmaking who's who all gathered at the Sherman Hotel in downtown Chicago for a gala send-off before boarding the Universal train headed for Hollywood. After a short stop in Denver, Colorado, where the guests took a tour of the city, the Universal train had a layover in Albuquerque, New Mexico; while there, they visited the Universal Theater. This nickelodeon booked only Universal pictures that were put out at a furious pace so that small theaters could show three short films and allowed them to change out their billboards daily. While in Albuquerque, the group visited a Pueblo Indian village and attended a grand banquet at the Savoy Hotel. One of the highlights for the Universalites, and most especially for Laemmle, who was himself a rebel at heart, was when Confederate officer—and the man who gave the order for the first shots to be fired against Fort Sumter at the outset of the Civil War—Henry Saxon Farley met the group and joined them for their banquet. Another thrill for the passengers when they arrived in Albuquerque was when buffalo hunter and scout William F. "Buffalo Bill" Cody met the train as it pulled into the station. Cody had gained fame for his Wild West show, which featured a rodeo, gunfights between cowboys and Indians and shooting and marksmanship exhibitions by the likes of Annie Oakley and Cody himself.

After the festivities in Albuquerque, the Universal train made a brief stop at the Grand Canyon before heading to San Bernardino, where it arrived on March 13. The following day, the Universalites visited Busch Gardens in Pasadena, California. Laemmle used this day to send and receive messages, making sure that all of the preparations were set and in order for the following day. Carl wanted to make sure that there would be no foul-ups to get in the way of his grand opening—too much was at stake. He had too much riding on this to leave anything to chance.

As the Universal train pulled into Los Angeles's Union Station on Monday morning, March 15, 1915, guitars and ukuleles began to play, and as the Universalites stepped onto the platform, they were greeted by all manner of actors and actresses in costumes depicting the guests' favorite movies and shorts. After six days of sightseeing and being cooped up on a train, when the travelers heard the music, they broke out into spontaneous dancing on the arrival platform. The *Los Angeles Times* reported it this way: "At the Santa Fe station here, the entire population of Universal Indians, band, cowboys and actors and actresses were gathered in welcoming enthusiasm and small arms salvos and a ukulele chorus accomplished a tantrum of noise that brought East First Street to the fore." So far as Laemmle could tell, the day's festivities couldn't have started any better.

Once the spur-of-the-moment festivities were at an end, the Universalites boarded buses and headed the few remaining miles to the hills just north

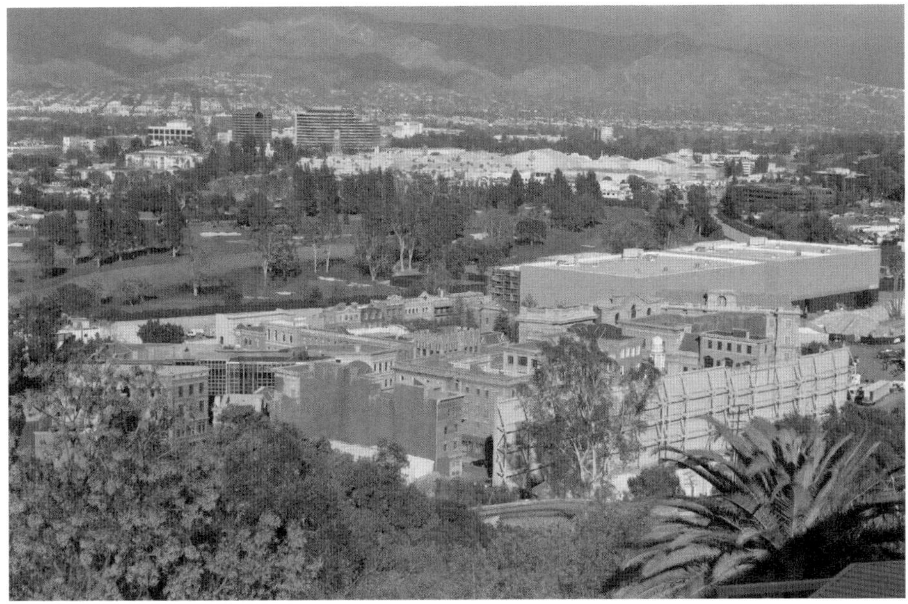

The famous back lot of Universal Studios as it looks today. You can see the Warner Bros. Studio in the background.

of Hollywood, where the gates of the new Universal City stood waiting for them. The group was dropped off on Lankershim Boulevard and, with Carl Laemmle leading the way, walked the short distance to where Universal City's mayor, police chief and commissioners were gathered to greet them as an honor guard of sorts. Even though the governing board comprised elected members, since Universal City was never an actual incorporated municipality, all of the twenty-eight elected positions were considered honorary. As California granted women the right to vote in 1911, of the twenty-eight people elected to the administration of Universal, ten positions went to suffragettes, including actress Grace Cunard, who was elected city assessor, and Laura Oakley, who was voted in as police chief.

On opening day, the estimated crowd was roughly ten thousand strong. Most of the guests arrived by bus, but an astonishing five hundred cars were parked in the dirt lot just outside the gates. This may not sound like a lot today, but in 1915, Los Angeles was not yet a city devoted to its car culture—most citizens either used public transport or horse-drawn buggies and wagons. The number of automobiles that showed up for this two-day event is phenomenal. The crowd cheered as Carl Laemmle strode up to the gate, holding high the keys that would unlock the gate to "the strangest city in the world," as it was dubbed by the press. With Chief of Police Laura Oakley, Mayor A.M. Kennedy (who also was the studio manager) and some of Universal's biggest stars by his side, Laemmle made a show of unlocking the gate and, with a grand flourish, throwing it wide.

There was a controlled rush to get inside to see what "Uncle Carl" had created. As with every phase of the grand opening, everything was done to amaze the public. There were barkers placed along Main Street, directing people where to go. They were purposely funneled past things that they were meant to see: the new outdoor stage, the unfinished studio commissary—which had a sign poking fun at Universal's own movie *The Great Universal Mystery* reading THE GREAT HASH MYSTERY—and past sets that were put up to give the crowd just a taste of moviemaking. Laemmle also wanted the guests to know that what he had created was indeed his own city, so the crowd was paraded past the city's post office, bank, schoolhouse and zoo. He purposely left out showing them the living area but made sure they were well aware of it. They did catch fleeting glimpses of the Native American living area—this was done to get them ready for the western show that they were going to see as soon as they arrived at the viewing stands.

As soon as the crowds arrived at the viewing area (it was standing room only), they were greeted by the sight of a fully loaded stagecoach slowly making its way toward them. The stagecoach, still a fair distance away, was clearly visible to all, and as they watched, a loud noise and a cloud of dust arose from behind a small hill. The dust was caused by over a dozen horses, ridden by the Universal Indians, and the noise was their war cry as they attacked the peaceful stagecoach. The driver urged the horses into a full gallop, but the attacking Indians were clearly gaining and now began to fire their rifles, trying to stop the fleeing settlers. The crowd gasped as the stagecoach reached the western town erected in front of the grandstands, and the townsfolk came out to see what was going on. The Indians, seeing the town come alive, began to fire on the citizens, and many of them went down in a hail of gunfire. The men of the town drew their own pistols and rifles and fought back. The crowd cheered with each Indian that was hit and fell from his horse as the settlers slowly gained the advantage and the attacking Indians fled or surrendered. Then, the show was over, and the guests clapped as loud as they could and again cheered their heroes. They applauded as the Indians arose or rode back to town to take their bow, and there was not a face in the crowd not wearing a smile. Carl Laemmle wore the biggest grin, as he realized that the first day of his two-day grand opening was a tremendous success. The only mar on an otherwise wonderful day was when pilot Frank Stites had to cancel his aerobatics and flying stunts when the wind became too strong for his biplane to take off. Laemmle, however, promised that Stites's exploits would go on the following day.

March 16, 1915, started with a little less fanfare than the opening day celebration, but the crowds that showed up at the gates of Universal City hadn't diminished in the least. Thousands of spectators came to see what Uncle Carl had in store for them on this, the second day of his grand opening party. Western films were the most popular in the early days of the cinema and, as luck would have it, the easiest to produce. Carl knew how important these films were, so he planned a whole day in which his guests could not only watch how they were filmed but also get up close and personal with the cowboys themselves. Universal had hired about thirty cowboys to work in the various pictures that were always being filmed and had most of them wandering around entertaining the crowd with rope tricks, wrangling and horsemanship—there was even a full-blown rodeo the guests could watch. One of the things that many of the guests had noticed was the odd arrangement of the city itself. While sitting and watching the Wild West shows and rodeos they could imagine themselves actually sitting in the wild west of the past, then, a quick look right and they were staring at the back of Tudor-style buildings like those found in old England, while a glance left caused you to be transported to Moscow and a Russian Orthodox church. Looking at this varied landscape with scenery from all over the world, one could fully understand why the press had dubbed Universal City "the strangest place on Earth."

The main event for the festivities this day was Frank Stites flying aerobatics. Having had to cancel his flight on opening day, Frank was anxious to show the crowd what he could do. Frank believed that for him to remain a competitive flyer, he would have to keep up with the Curtiss Exhibition Flying Team. One of its members had tragically died just two days earlier while attempting a stunt in San Francisco when his plane's wings had broken away and he plummeted into the bay. Frank knew that something like that could happen any time he took to the air, but like most young pilots, he figured it would never happen to him. On this day, Frank was to perform a series of loops, plunges and various other stunts, culminating in a mock attack on another aircraft. This other plane was actually on wires, strung between poles out of sight and rigged with explosives. Stites was supposed to attack the plane and, when directly overhead, drop a dummy "bomb" on the craft that would explode. Afterward, Stites was to perform a victory barrel roll. Stites was given the signal from the ground to proceed with his bomb

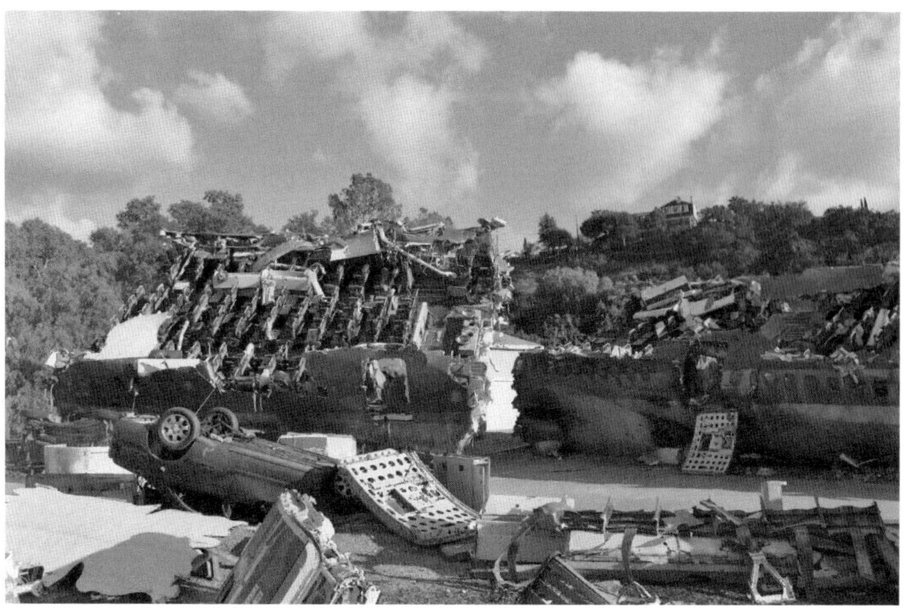

It was near this area where Frank Stites's body fell to the ground on day two of the grand opening ceremonies.

drop and made a perfect run on the mock plane—the replica airplane was set to explode when Stites's cloth-and-twine bomb got close—but the explosion was stronger than expected, and the concussion caused Stites to lose control of his airplane. Stites and his craft were now in freefall, with Frank trying everything his training told him to do, but to no avail. When Stites realized that it was a lost cause and his plane was going to crash, he attempted to jump to safety. He was still sixty feet from the ground, and when his body made impact, he was instantly killed. This would not be the last anyone heard from Frank Stites, however. It would seem that even though his career as a stunt pilot was over—as well as his life—he was not yet ready to retire.

The tragic and deadly accident that second day of the festivities took most of the joy out of the rest of the celebration, and Carl Laemmle decided to end the event early. Not wanting to disappoint his guests and send them away with a sour taste over the death, Laemmle, ahead of schedule, loaded his Universalites onto a train and sent them to end their epic journey at the San Francisco Panama-Pacific Exhibition. Even with the accident, both Laemmle and the public considered the grand opening of the world's first, largest and only dedicated, self-contained movie studio a complete success.

3

MAGIC, MONSTERS AND WAR

While Carl Laemmle was opening his City of Make Believe, the war in Europe was heating up. Germany, France and Britain were at a standstill in the trenches, Russia was falling back and all of Europe and parts of the Middle East were aflame with death and dying. Even though the United States was adamantly neutral, most, if not all of America was on the side of France and thought of Germany as the evil Hun empire, the enemy. Laemmle was torn between his home country of Germany and his loyalty to the United States. Because he had made himself a public figure, most of America had been following his every move. The country knew that Laemmle visited his hometown of Laupheim annually and had a habit of employing German directors, using German scripts and promoting German actors, such as Erich von Stroheim. Laemmle always referred to himself as an American but never denied or shied away from his German roots. After the war started, the American public began to perceive him as a German-American—with the hyphen being a problem—and not desirable to the public.

In an effort to change the image of both Universal Pictures and himself, Laemmle produced a series of films designed as antiwar propaganda against Germany. The first of these films, *The Sinking of Lusitania*, in 1918 portrayed Germans as the stereotypical Huns seen in cartoons throughout the war. Laemmle wanted to associate Germany with the brutality and barbarism of war and as the invading totalitarian conquerors. In another film, *The Kaiser: The Beast of Berlin*, Laemmle made Kaiser Wilhelm out to be Lucifer himself and the German army as spawns from hell. The films did have the effect that Laemmle wanted, and the American population began to see that Laemmle and Universal Pictures were not the enemy. Universal's releases were again making money at the box office. In Germany, however, even once the war was over, Uncle Carl was now a man shunned by even his old hometown. After the war, Laemmle visited his boyhood home of Laupheim and was greeted by protesting citizens who told Laemmle to leave and never return.

Once Carl returned to the United States, he led a campaign to aid Germany's reconstruction and, by using the power of Universal Pictures, gathered large amounts of cash and aid in the form of workers, material and other necessities needed for everyday life. Laemmle did this not only as a way to get back into the good graces of Germany's moviegoing population but also because he truly cared about people he still thought of as kin. All was going well with Laemmle's attempts at healing the wounds between Universal Pictures and his home country until the release of what is arguably the greatest movie the studio has ever produced, *All Quiet on the Western Front.* The movie won the Oscar for Best Picture in 1930, but in Germany, all of the reviews were negative, and the fledgling Nazi Party organized protests in front of movie theaters around the country. After only three days, the movie was banned in Germany. Laemmle thought that even though the movie showed the horrors of war it also portrayed the German people in a good light. Unfortunately, and with the help of master propagandist Joseph Goebbels, the German people disagreed, and Laemmle and Universal were once again on the outs with his home nation.

As much as Carl Laemmle wanted to make amends with Germany, he never lost sight of what his company's mission truly was: to make movie magic. The rise of his studio and its popularity can be traced to the studio's embracing of the moviegoing public. Almost immediately after the opening of Universal Studios, Laemmle had grandstands and bleachers erected around and near the stages and film locations on the lot. He invited the public to come and see the marvel of Hollywood moviemaking for a nominal fee of only twenty-five cents. Guests could even spend an extra five cents for a chicken box lunch. As the guests sat and watched their favorite movie stars perform in westerns, dramas or light-hearted comedies, they were encouraged to boo the bad guys, cheer the heroes and whistle, clap and jeer to their hearts' content. Laemmle realized that the number of people who could come and watch his films being made was small, but he also knew that the word-of-mouth advertising, along with the moderate amount of income generated by the spectators, was worth the minor annoyance of having hangers-on wandering around the studio.

In 1922, the studio was renamed Universal Pictures Corporation, and even though the studio was still producing low-budget westerns and melodramas, the 1920s saw the arrival of two notable classics. In 1923, Universal released *The Hunchback of Notre Dame* starring Lon Chaney and directed by Wallace Worsley. This film achieved great financial success for Universal, and the critical acclaim it received permanently established Universal as a premier Hollywood studio. The second film, also starring Lon Chaney, was *The Phantom of the Opera*, released in 1925. This film featured a large cast of studio favorites, and Chaney received critical acclaim for his portrayal of Erik, the disfigured man who hides out in the opera house. Chaney received accolades for his acting as well as his amazing makeup work, the likes of which had never been seen before. The entire opera house set was actually built right into sound stage 28, which over the years, until just recently, was used in many other movies and TV shows. This sound stage was one of the most haunted sites at the studio.

The 1920s was a frustrating decade for Universal Pictures. The company, unlike most other studios of the time, did not have the advantage of being

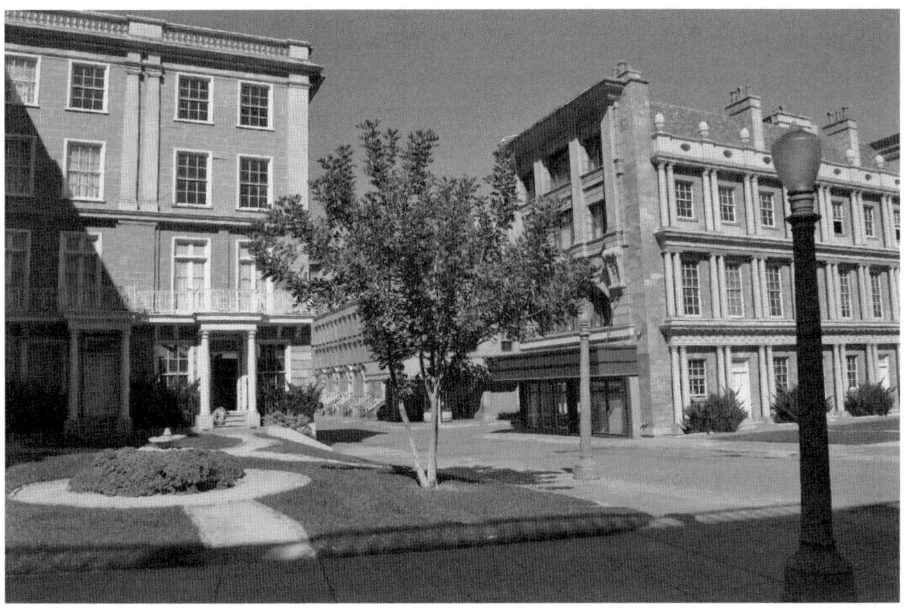

The sprawling back lot is made up of buildings that are nothing more than façades made to look like city blocks and brownstones.

affiliated with or ownership of a theater chain, where most first-run movies were shown in major cities throughout America. Universal relied on independent, rural theaters, and so the movies it produced catered to the tastes of rural audiences. Universal also accessed European markets, where American westerns and action movies found a large, enthusiastic audience. Through all of the turmoil of the times, Universal Studios grew, and those lucky enough to attend the filming watched as streets, building façades and whole towns grew seemingly overnight. The cathedral of Notre Dame overlooked a western town, a Monte Carlo casino stood near a New York skyline and a Paris opera house arose for all to see. One patron of the studio was quoted as saying, "Every time we come back to watch a new film being made, it's as if the whole world had appeared in Los Angeles as if by magic."

With the destruction of war still fresh in the minds of the world's population, Carl Laemmle figured he would give his audience something to distract them from what they had just gone through while allowing them to grieve and remember. Laemmle thought that the horror movie was the perfect way to accomplish this. The first ones on this list were the aforementioned *Hunchback of Notre Dame* and *The Phantom of the Opera*, followed by a string of classic horror and mystery films. Films such as *The Man Who Laughs*, *The Cat and the Canary* and *The Last Performance* gave the moviegoing public exactly what they needed to both forget about the horrors of World War I and replace their hatred of the Germans with fear of monsters on the silver screen. It also set Universal Pictures on the path to becoming the foremost authority on the art of the horror film, something that even to this day it has never relinquished.

Laemmle had always strived to make Universal Pictures into a studio where his films would become masterpieces and would go on to become classics in history. He was credited with producing Hollywood's first million-dollar production with the 1922 film *Foolish Wives.* The movie was a hit in America and parts of Europe, but because of Erich von Stroheim's involvement, it was a complete flop in Germany and other Germanic countries. Von Stroheim was still thought of as a propagandist, and therefore, anything he had a hand in was felt to be just more anti-German rhetoric. Other films produced in the decade went on to receive acclaim from American and European moviegoers, and it showed in the box office receipts. Movies such as *Marry-Go-Round* and *Les Misérables*, with their lavish sets, international stars and famous European directors, helped change the image of Universal Pictures from the cheap, low-budget western studio to a classic, masterpiece-producing Hollywood powerhouse. Universal continued to allow guests to attend the filming on the back lots and sets, and because of this, Universal's fame grew immensely—Carl Laemmle couldn't have been more pleased.

With the advent of talkies in the late 1920s, Universal found that the studio's policies would need to change. The investment in the new technologies, editing, soundtracks and even distribution were affected by the new format. Actors and actresses who were once the go-to stars for the studio now found themselves in unfamiliar territory, and many of them could not make the transition to speaking parts and were forced to leave the business. Universal's first talkie was the 1928 film *Melody of Love*, starring Walter Pidgeon.

Laemmle had difficulty transitioning from the silent era into the modern craze of sound pictures. He was unwilling to give up silent film theaters and believed that they would be around for a long time; because of this, Laemmle came up with a dual strategy of producing all of Universal's films in both sound and silent formats. This two-version approach meant that viewers have their silent pictures while the new generation was also served. Unfortunately, the cost associated with this approach was all but unsustainable.

When Carl Laemmle Jr. took over as general manager in charge of production in 1929, he adopted a more sophisticated approach to producing films. Laemmle Jr. fully embraced the talking picture format and slowly moved away from the silent era—and not a moment too soon. When the stock market crash hit on October 29, 1929, Universal was able to sustain itself, but just barely. The younger Laemmle cut the studio's output by 40 percent but concentrated on longer, higher-quality films. It was under Laemmle Jr.'s tutelage that the studio embarked on its now famous horror film crusade.

Even though the horror genre did well at the box office, the other films that Laemmle was now producing did not seem to capture the interest of the moviegoing public, and the box office take did not even out the high cost of production for Universal's feature films. One such film being produced was the now classic *Showboat*. This movie remake of the hit Broadway show produced by Laemmle Jr. in 1935 ran so over budget that it literally broke the bank at the studio. Knowing that Universal needed capital to keep operating, Carl did something he swore he would never do: he sought out a loan to keep the studio running. There is some discrepancy in the amount borrowed, ranging from $750,000 to just over $1 million, but regardless of the actual amount, Laemmle put the studio up as collateral for the loan. As the costs rose higher and higher for the film, it became clear to Carl that he would have trouble paying off the debt, as the release date of *Showboat* kept being delayed. By 1936, the Executive Board of Universal was getting worried about the leadership of the Laemmle family, and the investors called in their option. This allowed Standard Capital to acquire Laemmle's shares of Universal Pictures for $4.1 million, ending an era at Universal Studios. Laemmle was heartbroken at the fact that he had to leave the studio that he had built and run for over two decades. His final speech as he left the now largest and most influential studio in Hollywood was filled with both regret and hope for the future of Universal Pictures.

Carl Laemmle was never one to rest on his laurels, and after he was forced to sell Universal Pictures, he dedicated his life to helping those affected by the rise of Hitler and the Nazis in his home country. He was no longer allowed in Germany due to the release of *All Quiet on the Western Front* but remained in contact with his family in Laupheim as well as friends he had made during his tenure at Universal and former employees. He was well aware of the worsening conditions facing Jews, and Laemmle personally sponsored more than three hundred Jewish families so they could immigrate to the United States. Once it became clear that he had exhausted the possibility of obtaining more sponsorships himself, he appealed to his family, friends, former employees and many others he had come to know throughout the years to help sponsor many more. His steadfast support of European Jews was in direct contrast to the rest of Hollywood's Jewish producers, including Adolph Zukor of Paramount, and Louis B. Meyer over at MGM. Zukor is quoted as saying, "I don't think that Hollywood should deal with anything but entertainment. The news reels take care of current events. To make films of political significance is a mistake." What a far cry that position takes in comparison with the radical political stances taken by studios and movie stars today. Laemmle, however, could not just idly stand by and watch as Hitler slowly put the Jews of Germany into the categories of either slaves or animals. The month before Kristallnacht, or the Night of Broken Glass, where Nazi Stormtroopers destroyed Jewish shops, synagogues and buildings and dragged hundreds of Jews off to jail on trumped-up charges, Laemmle had written to his nephew Willian Wyler about his concerns for what was happening in his beloved Germany:

> *Dear Mr. Wyler, I want to ask you a very big favor. The Jewish situation in Germany has been getting on my nerves for a long, long time. I feel these poor, unfortunate people need help in the worst way. I have been over there*

> *and know what they are going through. I have issued so many personal affidavits that the United States government won't accept any more from me except from my closest blood relatives. Nevertheless, while I was over there, I was worried so much by the distressed people that I promised about 150 of them I would move heaven and Earth to find sponsors for them. This is why I am writing you this letter.*

With the help of his nephew and his former protégé, Paul Kohner, Laemmle formed an anti-Nazi stronghold in Hollywood. Wyler, now an immigrant to the United States himself, became one of the leading film directors in Hollywood and joined the U.S. Army Air Corps, flying B-17 bombers against his former home country.

Carl Laemmle passed away in Los Angeles from a massive heart attack in 1939 at the age of seventy-two. His funeral, like his life, became a celebration of all that was Hollywood and all that could be accomplished if one simply strove to achieve. Say what you will about Uncle Carl Laemmle, but without his guidance and leadership, Hollywood would not be what it is today. He took on one of the most powerful men in the world and won. Perhaps the greatest testament to Laemmle is that the man who was once his enemy, Thomas Edison, came to admire and appreciate what Laemmle had built. When Laemmle opened up a new chapter in the Universal saga, Edison was there to dedicate the new state-of-the-art electric studio.

4
THE MAGIC CHANGES HANDS

Nepotism had always been a problem at Universal Pictures. It was so well known that Carl Laemmle liked to hire any and all family members who asked for a job that famed poet Ogden Nash quipped, "Uncle Carl Laemmle has such a very large faemmle." It was this rampant nepotism, along with a few bad decisions by Carl Laemmle Jr., that put an end to the Laemmle era at the studio. When Carl Laemmle failed to meet the financial obligations of the loan he had taken out to keep the studio running, Standard Capital foreclosed, forcing Laemmle to sell his interest in the company for $4.1 million.

Under Standard, the studio became known as New Universal, and one of the first things it did was shut down all of the studio's European holdings and operations. Carl Laemmle had already shut down the tours and public viewing of productions at the studio when it became clear that the talkies would not allow audiences. With too much noise and interference from the crowds, Laemmle had no choice but to stop the public spectacles. This was just fine with Standard, as it thought the public would have been an insurance liability anyway. These, along with other drastic cost-cutting measures, helped keep Universal from complete ruin. In an odd twist of fate, two films begun before the Laemmle ouster, *My Man Godfrey* and *Three Smart Girls*, were also credited with saving the studio from bankruptcy. The star of *Three Smart Girls*, fifteen-year-old Deanna Durbin, became one of the studio's biggest stars. In her tenure at Universal Pictures, Durbin would star in no fewer than twenty-one movies. In 1938, Durbin received a special

Oscar from the Academy of Motion Pictures for "bringing youthfulness to the silver screen." There are many who claim that it was Durbin alone who should get the credit for saving Universal Pictures. Another irony is the fact that when *Showboat*, the film that led to the ouster of the Laemmles was finally released, it became a box office success and helped pull Universal back into the limelight. Because production had begun before Standard had taken control of the studio, the Laemmles' names are both featured in the credits for production.

As two new executives came on board in the late 1930s, the company again cut costs. It was the leadership's hope that the studio could still put out above-average feature films to sate the more discerning audiences while producing its standard low-budget westerns, serials, comedies and horror films. With the help of Durbin's movies, a surprising return on the film *Destry Rides Again*—starring James Stewart and Marlene Dietrich—and the box office success of *Showboat*, Universal Pictures was able to go from the brink of bankruptcy in 1936 to a substantial profit of around $1.5 million.

When World War II erupted in Europe, it became clear that the United States and the rest of the world craved an escape. Since most of the world was on fire, motion pictures became the most obvious way for the public to affect this retreat from the reality of a world gone mad. Universal Pictures was more than happy to help facilitate this escape. The dynamic comedy duo of Bud Abbott and Lou Costello debuted in 1940 with *One Night in the Tropics*, and the two became one of the most popular draws for audiences throughout the war, as well as one of the greatest comedy teams of all time. Many will remember this film for its iconic "Who's on First?" routine. Other popular films made during the war were thirteen war-themed musicals featuring the Andrews Sisters as well as *The Adventures of Sherlock Holmes* and *Inner Sanctum* mysteries. Of course, monster movies were still a big draw for the studio, which produced more than thirty of these films during the war years.

Universal had always relied on low-budget films and, as such, was one of the last studios to use the new three-strip Technicolor process employed by all of the other movie studios. The new process was expensive but produced superb, vivid color, which gave the films that much more appeal to the moviegoing public. One of the first films in which Universal employed Technicolor was the 1942 release of *Arabian Nights*, starring Jon Hall and Maria Montez. The response Universal received from moviegoers prompted the studio to use the new process the following year for the remake of the classic *Phantom of the Opera*, starring Claude Rains, Nelson Eddy and Susanna

Foster. This again proved to be very popular with the moviegoing public and prompted Universal to finally sign a contract with Technicolor and set a regular schedule of high-budget Technicolor films.

As World War II ended and the world tried to get back to normal, or as normal as possible, the population again turned to the movies for entertainment. The escape from the realities of war turned into a need for reassurance and a glimpse to the fun times that lay ahead in the wake of the new nuclear future. The moviegoing public demanded high-quality films if they were going to part with their hard-earned money. As a way to help facilitate this new demand, Universal merged with International Pictures in 1946 and renamed the studio Universal-International Pictures. International brought the experience of one of the two studios' chief rivals, as two of its heads, William Goetz and Leo Spitz, were both former executives of 20th Century Fox. One of the first things Goetz did was eliminate all serials, Arabian Nights sequels, B movie productions and, worst of all, Universal's horror movies from the production lineup. He felt that this would help bring prestige to the floundering company. Universal-International once again expanded into the European markets when it became responsible for American distribution of Rank's British productions and expanded farther when it aligned itself with Castle Films, a dealer in home movie distribution. In another cost-cutting move, Universal dropped several stars. This has always been a decision mired in controversy, as Universal had always had a problem getting stars into its stable of performers, so letting any of them go was a gamble. It did retain the contracts for Abbot and Costello, Durbin and Donald O'Connor.

Goetz had believed that producing higher-budget films with more lavish and elaborate sets would translate into higher box office takes. There were some films produced under Goetz's watch that became hits, such as *The Killers* or the 1948 classic *The Naked City* and, of course, the top-grossing film of 1947, *The Egg and I*, which brought in close to $6 million. But as the 1940s came to a close, it became clear that Universal-International was again operating at a loss. The model that Goetz had set for the studio was clearly not working, and he was promptly fired. Around the same time, the studio got some good news from the Supreme Court when it ruled in favor of independent theaters over the studios in a landmark antitrust case. Universal never built or owned proprietary theater chains and had always dealt with local, independent theater owners. Now that the court ruled that studios could no longer own their own theaters and had to distribute their movies to other chains, Universal knew it would take time for the other studios to set up their distribution apparatus. Universal-Independent, having been set up this way all along, was now set to take advantage of the confusion that would ensue. Its revenue stream was safe.

Once Goetz was gone from the front office, the studio once again began producing its standard low-budget movies to complement the extravagant feature films. Low-cost films like the *Ma and Pa Kettle* series became popular, and the ten movies in the lineup were lucrative, as were the *Francis the Talking Mule* films starring Donald O'Connor, and these all helped Universal out of the slump. The 1950s saw the return of the *Arabian Nights* films, and many of these star Tony Curtis. Universal's monster and horror movies were making a comeback, complemented now by the new science fiction genre, which was becoming popular with American movie audiences. Universal-International was now sporting a stable of new talent that included Tony Curtis, Audie Murphy, Rock Hudson and Jeff Chandler, to name just a few. In a landmark deal that was to change the way contracts were designed in the movie industry, James Stewart's agent cut a deal with Universal-International in 1950 that gave Stewart a smaller salary but granted him a share in the profits. When the film *Winchester '73* became a big hit and its profits soared, this new contract arrangement became the norm not only for Universal but the other studios as well. Again, Universal led the way for modernization in Hollywood.

The 1952 acquisition of Universal-International by Decca Records brought another change to the philosophy and the name of Universal Pictures. With Milton Rackmil as president of the company, gross receipts increased $7 million by 1954, and lesser known independent producers were brought in to make movies at the studio. This new idea succeeded when the films *The Incredible Shrinking Man*, *Touch of Evil* and *The Glenn Miller Story*, along with *Operation Petticoat*, became big hits for the studio. Other movies that came out at this time that were highly successful and produced by independents were *Imitation of Life*, starring Lana Turner, and *Pillow Talk*, with Rock Hudson and Doris Day.

By the late 1950s and early 1960s, it had become clear that audiences were changing. With the breakup of the theater/studio chain monopoly, people were able to go to any theater they chose for movies, which reduced the overall size of the crowd at any given movie house. The gains that Universal had seen in its revenue stream due to the court order had slowly dwindled, as the other studios gained back their market share and with the advent of television, many of those who once made the Saturday night pilgrimage to the

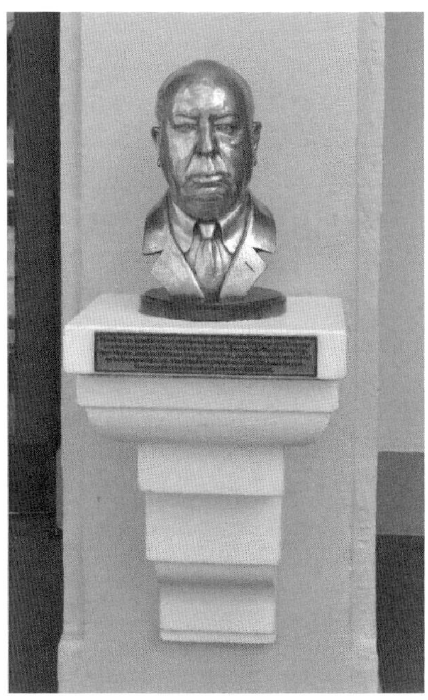

Alfred Hitchcock was so important to the success of Universal Studios that the studio erected a bust of the director just inside the gates of the theme park.

movie theater were now staying home. From a profit of $4 million in 1956 and 1957, Universal lost $2 million in 1958 alone. As a whole, the combined loss to the movie industry was a 12 percent decline in ticket sales at the box office. Beginning in 1957, Universal leased 550 of its earlier movies, all made before 1948, to Screen Gems for the television market. Even with this new revenue stream, Universal was struggling to keep afloat. In an effort to keep the creditors at bay, Universal sold its studio lot to the Music Corporation of America (MCA) for $11.25 million; it did not, however, sell Universal Pictures. MCA was the world's largest talent agency and the company that had negotiated James Stewart's profit sharing contract; it was becoming one of the largest television producers in the world with its Revue Television Productions arm, which produced the hit show *Leave It to Beaver*. MCA merged with Decca Records in 1962, and the studio changed its name once again, this time to MCA Universal.

One of the first things MCA did once it had complete control was to completely upgrade and modernize the studio and back lot. MCA also signed some of its biggest clients to film contracts. Names like Cary Grant, Lana Turner and Doris Day became regulars at the commissary, and director Alfred Hitchcock had his own office on the lot. Even after Hitchcock died, he hung around, giving Steven Spielberg directing tips. In 1964, MCA completely removed itself from its talent agency commitments and signed as many of its clients to contracts with Universal as was feasible. This was also the year that the company reinstated the tours of Universal City. Some of the movies released during this time were the blockbuster *To Kill a Mockingbird* and Alfred Hitchcock's classic thriller *The Birds*. *To Kill a Mockingbird* won three Academy Awards, including the Best Actor nod for Gregory Peck.

The 1960s ended with a bang for MCA Universal with the hit movie *Thoroughly Modern Millie* in 1968 and started the 1970s off right with the star-studded *Airport*, which grossed just over $45 million. The success of these movies set the trend for Universal Pictures for the next decade, with 1973 as the stand-out year. It was this year that *The Sting* was released, grossed $79 million at the box office and won seven Academy Awards, including Best Picture. *American Graffiti* received four nominations and grossed $57 million, and *The Day of the Jackal* and Clint Eastwood's haunting portrayal of the no-name gunslinger in *High Plains Drifter* were highly acclaimed movies from that same year. Another film that was highly successful but not that well received by the Academy was the disaster flick *Earthquake*. This was another of those star-heavy movies in the *Airport* tradition of the 1970s that became known as the disaster film genre.

In 1975, Universal released the movie *Jaws*, and it became the highest grossing film of all time, with fans flocking to the theaters and many seeing the movie multiple times. *Jaws* would go on to make a whopping $133 million. Other fan favorites from the 1970s were *Smoky and the Bandit*, starring Burt Reynolds and Sally Field, *National Lampoon's Animal House* and *The Blues Brothers*. These last two films, although not huge box office successes, became cult favorites with large followings and made Dan Aykroyd and John Belushi household names. Steven Spielberg would go on to make some of the most well received and highly acclaimed movies to come out of Universal Pictures, such as *E.T. the Extra-Terrestrial* and the *Back to the Future* films with Robert Zemeckis.

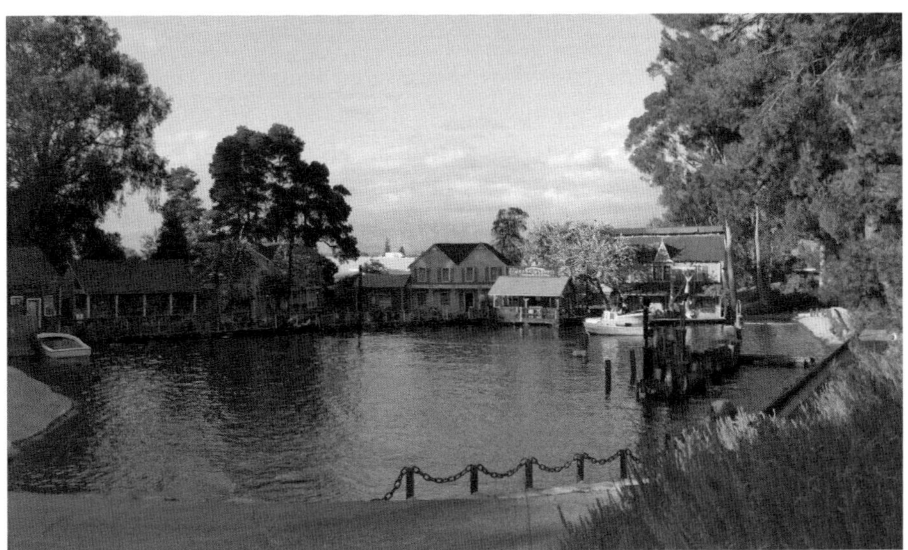

"Amity Island." The fictional hunting ground of the great white shark from the movie *Jaws*.

Moving into the 1980s, Universal again took on the task of expanding its facilities. With the addition of 220 acres, Universal City again became the largest studio lot in Hollywood. Among the new accompaniments were a fourteen-story administration building, thirty-six new sound stages, a Technicolor film laboratory and a 200,000-square-foot complex to accommodate independent producers. After Steven Spielberg started his Amblin Entertainment production company, he moved out of Hitchcock's old office and into one of these bungalows.

Even though Universal was putting out numerous blockbusters and fan-favorite movies, it was fully involved with television productions as well; as a matter of fact, TV still made up much of the studio's output. Hit shows such as *The Jeffersons*, *Silver Spoons*, *One Day at a Time* and the highly popular *Diff'rent Strokes* were some of the biggest moneymakers for the studio. The National Broadcasting Company (NBC) was Universal's biggest client; the studio provided half of the network's prime-time lineup. One of the new things happening in television at this time was the made-for-television movie. Universal dove headfirst into this new media and helped produce many classic television films.

Anxious to break into the new cable medium growing around the country and wanting to expand its broadcast presence, MCA head Lew Wasserman approached Japanese electronics giant Matsushita Electronics—known by its Panasonic brand name in the United States—and the company agreed to acquire MCA for $6 billion in 1990. The reason Wasserman needed the buyout was to bring in a large infusion of capital to expand into the new cable market. Unfortunately, the Japanese were not prepared to deal with the culture of Hollywood and sold the majority share in Universal (80 percent) to the Canadian Seagram Company. This merger didn't last long. After Seagram was purchased by PolyGram, the newest owners found that profits just weren't what they thought they would be, so Seagram was then sold to the French company Vivendi. Within four years, Vivendi also found itself in trouble and sold 80 percent of its Universal holdings to General Electric, parent company of NBC. By 2011, Comcast had acquired NBC and become the current NBCUniversal trademark that we know today. Even with the turmoil of the 1990s and early 2000s, Universal seems poised to remain the premier studio in Hollywood and maintain its dominance as one of the top tourist draws and theme parks in all of California.

5
The Monster Mash

It's hard to think about Universal Studios without also thinking about monsters. The reason for this, although most people don't realize it, is that Universal created the most iconic monsters of all time. Frankenstein's Monster, the Mummy, Count Dracula, the Wolf Man and the Creature from the Black Lagoon are all Universal's children. The filmmakers may not have created the characters, but at the very least, Universal created the image of the characters that we all know them by today. Every Halloween, walking down every street in North America you will see the image of Dracula that originated from Bela Lugosi's performance or the flat-headed, bolt-necked Frankenstein's Monster that Boris Karloff implanted in the consciousness of the world in the movie *Frankenstein.* Everybody that grew up in America, dare I say the world, watched any number of shows and movies that had one of these highly recognizable creatures stalking its victims and being pursued by townsfolk. Say what you will, but monsters are as American as apple pie.

Universal began releasing horror films almost from day one of its creation. In 1913, the studio released two such films: *Dr. Jekyll and Mr. Hyde*, starring King Baggot, and *The Werewolf*, starring Phyllis Gordon as an Indian witch who can transform into a wolf. Although neither of these movies were ever highly popular and have now fallen into obscurity (*The Werewolf* is now considered a "lost film"), they were nonetheless a foretelling of things to come. The first horror films to become hits for Universal came in 1923 when the studio released its version of the *The Hunchback of Notre Dame* and then again with the 1925 release of *The Phantom of the Opera.*

In the early days of Hollywood, there were no makeup departments, no on-call artists to come and turn the actors and actresses into the unflawed masks of beauty or the horrific bad guys and villains of western lore and fright films. Up until sometime in the mid-1920s, every actor or actress was required to apply his or her own makeup and create his or her own persona for the characters the performer was hired to play. Lon Chaney, knowing this, took it upon himself to learn all he could about makeup, how it could be applied, manipulated and changed to create anyone or anything he wanted. This expert ability he developed not only gave him an advantage over other actors of the time but also led others into the field of makeup. which helped create the entire industry we know today. In *The Phantom of the Opera*, Chaney took the art of makeup to new and painful levels when, to create the desired revulsion when one looked at the Phantom, he placed hooks in his nostrils, ran wire up the bridge of his nose and pulled them tight behind his ears to get the distinctive flare we see on the screen. It was his dedication to the art that garnered him the nickname "Man of a Thousand Faces."

In *The Hunchback of Notre Dame*, Chaney created one of the most grotesquely deformed characters in the history of film, and his portrayal of the love-struck Quasimodo, the deaf bell ringer of Notre Dame, is one that truly brings out the monster's innate humanity. Then, in 1925, Chaney stunned and terrified the audience with the hideously disfigured face of Erik, the phantom, in a way that had never been seen on the screen up to that point. In the posters and promos for the film, Universal made sure to hide the face of the phantom so that when his visage was finally revealed in the movie, it would have the biggest effect possible on the viewer. Another reason for the popularity of *Phantom of the Opera* had to do with the realism of the film or, more specifically, the realism of the sets. Universal actually built the entire opera house, stage, balconies and theater boxes right into sound stage 28. This stage was one of the biggest in Hollywood, and Universal would use the opera house over and over again in many movies. Lon Chaney loved this set so much, maybe due to him spending so much time there, that even after his death, he returns often enough that his spirit has become a common sight to actors and crew who still work the stage to this day. The box office take for these movies was huge, and it set Universal on a course that is still felt today.

When the new talkies arrived in the late 1920s and early 1930s, Universal was there to scare the moviegoing public with visual frights, dialogue and subtle innuendo provided by actors who would become the epitome of the horror genre. With the 1931 release of the movie *Dracula*, the audience was introduced to a new Count, one that was at the same time familiar to those who had seen the stage production and completely different than the menacing vampire from the 1922 classic *Nosferatu*. Bela Lugosi was brought over from the Broadway show to reprise his role for the movie, and his hypnotic stare and imposing stature immediately drew viewers into the dark sphere of the cunning Count. The way Lugosi plays Dracula, with his slow Hungarian accent and slightly menacing undertones mixes well with the not-so-hidden sadness that always seems to be just under the surface. Viewers are never quite sure if they should be scared of him, feel sorry for him or pray that he gets staked as soon as possible. *Dracula* was released before widespread censorship had reached the Hollywood studios, and the movie comes across as a sensual tour de force, at least for the period, and this, along with Lugosi's charm and mystery, make *Dracula* one of the first horror blockbuster movies ever made.

The same year that *Dracula* was released, Universal's adaptation of Mary Shelley's classic *Frankenstein* also came to the theaters. Universal had originally wanted to cast Bela Lugosi for the role of the monster but the film's director, James Whale, decided that an obscure actor by the name of Boris Karloff would be a better choice for the part. The idea was to make the monster an unfeeling, diabolical killing machine, but when the towering Karloff got to the set, Whale took one look at him, and the whole dynamic of the creature changed. The monster was transformed from a mindless killing zombie into an almost childlike and confused lost soul rather than a monstrous killer. It would seem that Whale wanted to get this point across to the audience with the now famous scene where the monster comes across the young girl by the lakeside and all he seems to want is to make a friend. Even though the scene ends badly, the motivation of the creature is clear. This theme of a lonely, scared child is repeated in the sequel when the monster is befriended by an old blind man. When vengeful townsfolk arrive, and the old man's house burns down around the creature, he mournfully cries out "friend," over and over again, hoping the old man will come back to him. This "monster with emotion" became a consistent theme in many of Universal's horror films.

Boris Karloff was again cast in the part of a Universal monster when he appeared in 1932's *The Mummy*. Regardless of the title, the film only features Imhotep's mummified corpse for a few moments in the opening scenes. But those brief clips as Imhotep is brought back to life and the surprised young archaeologist is driven mad by the sight of the cloth-wrapped priest set the tone for the rest of the film, which, as many viewers have stated, seems a bit of a letdown after such a terrifying introduction. Even though the film is light on the wrappings, Karloff's portrayal of Ardath Bey, Imhotep's modern persona, looking for his lost love Ankhesenamun in an attempt to resurrect her spirit caught the widespread attention of the moviegoing public. This was another example of Universal's propensity for making its creatures sympathetic. So popular and iconic was *The Mummy* that over the years, the franchise has had many sequels produced, cartoon mummies galore and a trilogy of films starring Brendan Fraser and Rachel Weisz. Now Universal is resurrecting the film with a woman in the starring role as the kick-off for its new Dark Universe series of monster movies.

With the successes of *Dracula*, *Frankenstein* and *The Mummy*, Universal set out to make a trilogy of films based on the writings of American horror author Edgar Allan Poe. *Murders in the Rue Morgue* was released in 1932 and followed by *The Black Cat* in 1934 and *The Raven* the following year. In between these films, Universal released *The Invisible Man*, starring Claude Rains. This is not your typical horror movie in which a monstrous creature roams the countryside looking for blood, rather it is a tale of one man's slide into madness and ego-driven megalomania as he realizes his complete anonymity (in his mind) by being invisible. The movie is more dark comedy than horror film, and Rains is masterful in the role. His delivery of some extremely black jokes and his playfulness as he plots his dastardly deeds is pure genius. This is also one of the first films to make extensive use of special effects. The director used blue screen technology, the precursor of today's modern green screen, and the scenes in which Rains is supposed to be on camera allow the audience to truly believe that he is there even though made invisible by the camera. The scene that has the (presumably naked) invisible man riding his bike down a country lane while whistling is hard not to find amusing, and watching him leave footprints in the snow (actually shoe prints in a blooper moment) add up to one rooting for the maniacal madman.

In 1935, James Whale bowed under pressure from Universal and reluctantly signed on to direct the very first horror sequel, *The Bride of Frankenstein.* Boris Karloff reprised his role as the monster from the original film and again plays the part less as a fiend and more as the lost little boy we remember—indeed, it seems as if most of the humans surrounding Karloff's character are more monstrous than the monster himself. Elsa Lanchester plays the title role and is uncredited for it. The Bride is only on screen for a few minutes, but Lanchester's performance is so haunting and her hair so recognizable that it is known all around the world to this day. Elsa Lanchester would go on to have a long, stellar career; however, it is for this role that she will always be remembered.

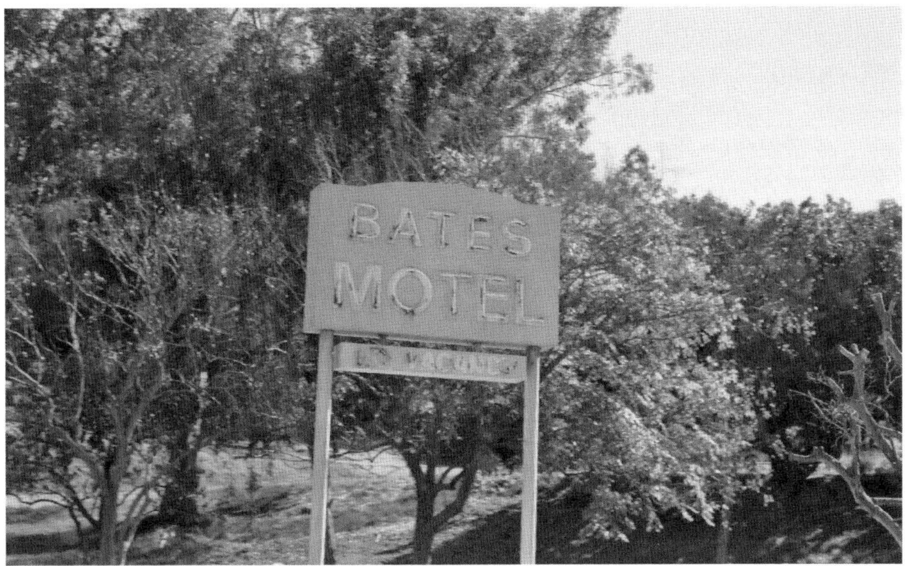

The Bates Motel murder scene in the movie *Psycho*, one of the most iconic horror films of the 1960s, kept people away from the shower for years.

After *The Bride of Frankenstein*, Universal continued to produce horror films, and many of them were box office hits; however, none of these produced what one would call an iconic character or monster—that is until the year 1941. Based on folklore and legend rather than literary works as much of the past Universal fare was, *The Wolf Man* could take any road its writer wanted it to follow, and that is exactly what Curt Siodmak did with his script. Lon Chaney Jr. was cast in the part of Larry Talbot, a spoiled second son of a wealthy lord who is called back from America after his older brother is killed; Larry is to take over as heir to the fortune. No sooner does Larry arrive than he gets bitten by Bela Lugosi and becomes a werewolf. Chaney was not one of the better actors in the Universal stable but suited the part well with his bumbling gait and blank expression before changing into the hairy wolf that we all recognize today. The tale is not simply a monster flick but a story of redemption and a father who would do anything to help his child. Again, Universal makes the audience not only cringe from the monster but also feel for the creature and almost root for his survival in the hopes that he and his father will again join together as true family should.

Universal spent the rest of the 1940s making sequel after sequel within the established monster pantheon. Movies such as *The Ghost of Frankenstein*, *The Mummy's Tomb*, *Son of Dracula*, *House of Dracula*, *Frankenstein Meets the Wolf*

Man and so on. Then, in 1948, Universal put a proverbial nail in the coffin of its established monsters; that year, *Abbott and Costello Meet Frankenstein* was released. The studio had been seeing a marked decline at the box office for its "Monster-Mash" movies as they were referred to in the media, and Universal had already decided to retire its old standbys. What better way to do this than to put them into a comedy with its highest-grossing duo, Abbott and Costello. Unfortunately, Boris Karloff would not reprise his role as the Monster; however, Bela Lugosi returned to play the role of the red and black–caped Count Dracula, and Lon Chaney Jr. returned as the Wolf Man. The film is set in Florida at a dark and scary gothic castle with a mad scientist's lab. In Florida? The plot is razor thin, with the whole film being nothing more than a vehicle for the comedy duo to perform sight gags. The monsters it would seem are only in the film as joke set-ups rather than frights; they are never made fun of or treated disrespectfully, but it is clear that this is a comedy movie and not a monster movie. This is why I say that it was the end of the monster era, at least temporarily; it's hard to get scared of a monster once you have laughed at it and with it, even if you are a kid. In *Abbott and Costello Meet the Invisible Man* and *Abbott and Costello Meet Dr. Jekyll and Mr. Hyde*, along with *Abbott and Costello Meet the Mummy*, those villains meet their doom as well.

After the horror of World War II and the dropping of the atomic bomb brought us into the nuclear age, along with the beginning of the Cold War, moviegoing audiences' tastes in horror films took a dramatic turn. No longer were the old gothic monsters of the past the frightening boogie men of the future—now, it was science gone wrong that scared the world. What diabolical fiends were being created by the ever-growing atomic test clouds? What horrors awaited the world from radiation gone astray, and what monsters would emerge from the toxic waste being spread by the governments of the world? This new fear of science was immediately picked up on by the movie and television studios, and B movies were being pumped out by the dozens; Universal was no exception.

One of Universal's first sci-fi horror attempts was the Ray Bradbury–inspired *It Came from Outer Space*. Not really a monster movie even with its giant-eyed space aliens, it touches on the country's fear of what we don't understand and the way mankind reacts with anger and hostility toward that which is foreign. The "monsters" in the film are treated as misunderstood creatures, and the audience is led, as is the Universal way, to sympathize and feel for the mistreated aliens. The film is, in its own way, quite scary and a worthy start to Universal's sci-fi pantheon.

Universal's next installment, *Creature from the Black Lagoon*, is another film that spawned a creature still highly recognizable to even the youngest trick-or-treater. This is another movie in which Universal gives us a creature that is not simply to be feared but sympathized with in a Beauty and the Beast tradition. The Gillman finds that he is smitten with the heroine of the film, Key Lawrence, played by Julie Adams, and even though he has already killed some of her companions in an effort to get them to leave his lagoon, he blocks them from escape and kidnaps Key and takes her to his cave. This ultimately leads to his supposed doom. There is a scene in the film in which the Gillman swims directly under Key, and the scene has an eerie beauty to it that makes the audience aware of the creature's feeling for the human woman. Again, Universal not only wanted the audiences to feel fear but also desired them to use their emotions of love, sympathy and, ultimately, loss.

With the exception of the 1956 film *The Mole People* and the highly recognizable underground mutant mushroom farmers, Universal didn't create another iconic monster until the Graboids came out in the 1990 release of *Tremors*, unless of course you place Bruce the Shark from the movie *Jaws* in the category of monster. One movie that must be mentioned is the 1960 film *Psycho*. This Alfred Hitchcock classic stars Anthony Perkins as the mentally disturbed Norman Bates. The movie has perhaps the most well-known shower scene in the history of cinema when embezzler Marion Crane, played by the beautiful Janet Leigh, is brutally knifed to death by a killer hidden behind the curtain in a bloody scene that had viewers afraid to take showers for years afterward. The character of Norman Bates would go on to be the poster child for insanity, and the movie would become the first in a long line of movies known collectively as slasher films. Another Hitchcock film that deserves an honorable mention is the 1963 thriller *The Birds*. Technically not a horror film but a suspense thriller, this movie had audiences on the edge of their seats in terror as thousands of seemingly innocuous birds decide to attack and kill any human being they encounter.

Universal Studios is in the process of resurrecting horror classics and even plans on combining them into a single universe in which they can interact. Why the studio feels the need for this is beyond this writers' comprehension, but it is exciting to think that the studio will be introducing a whole new generation to the classic horror pantheon. No matter who you are, young or old, it is an almost sure bet that you are at least familiar with most, if not all of Universal's classic horror monsters. After all, I'm pretty sure we all dressed up at Halloween as one of them when we were younger and may have nightmares about them still.

6
The Glamour Trams

From the moment that Carl Laemmle opened his studio in Hollywood, he knew that the public would be a big part of its success. He knew that his audience had a fascination with the movies and how they were made and knew that the stars of the films would always be a big draw. After all, who wouldn't want a chance to meet their afternoon idol in person? Visiting his new city would allow the fans to see how the movies were made and give them the chance to meet the stars of Hollywood face-to-face. Laemmle knew that this would help draw people to the movie palaces, and it also was a way for him to make more money by charging a small admission fee.

As early as 1912, when Laemmle opened the newly acquired Bison 101 film location at Oak Crest Ranch to guests, he knew he had a winning idea. Laemmle began charging five cents a person to enter the studio, and people began to come on a regular basis. There were even organized tours coming in from nearby Los Angeles. The crowds loved seeing the real Native Americans in their "natural element" and had so much fun cheering on the town sheriff or the white-hatted gunslinger out-drawing the bad guy that they didn't want to leave when the day of shooting was over. Once Laemmle opened his new Universal City, things began to change for the better, and the money would come in at a much greater rate.

After the grand opening of his new, state-of-the-art studio, Laemmle allowed guests to come see where the films were made, and he fed them—after all, his new city was a chicken ranch. Laemmle raised the price of admission to his movie city to twenty-five cents, but that price included a chicken lunch. Bleachers were set up around the outdoor stages, and if the small chicken lunch was not enough to sate their appetites, guests were encouraged to head over to the commissary, where they could purchase more. There was a good chance of running into movie stars enjoying their lunches, and this gave the guests an opportunity to rub elbows with the Hollywood elite.

Things were paying off splendidly for Universal. Box office sales were up, attendance at the studio was steady and profitable and the extra money coming from commissary service pushed the studio well into the black. Then came sound. Even though Universal was one of the last studios to embrace talking pictures, it was an inevitability that it would have to move into the future and that future was sound in cinema. Once the studio came to grips with this realization in the early 1930s, it also realized that it was no longer feasible to have spectators present during filming. Where once cheering from the crowd was a welcome sound, now it only ruined the scene. Directors found themselves having to constantly stop filming, trying to get the guests to be quiet on set only to have them once again ruin the shot with too much noise. Reluctantly, Universal Studios decided to end its tradition of the public watching the movies being made and stopped allowing guest to enter the lot. By 1935, with lower than expected earnings in both movie sales and possibly due to the loss of visitor entry fees and food sales, Laemmle was forced out, and the studio would go through numerous owners over the following decades. All thoughts of public tours seemed to die out with the Laemmles no longer on the scene.

It would take another twenty years before the general public would again be allowed to view the inside of the studio; this time, however, it would be as passengers aboard iconic Gray Line tour buses. Gray Line was a tour company that, in Hollywood, specialized in trips past movie stars' homes and studios such as Paramount, Warner Brothers and Disney. Knowing that Universal had once been open to the public, Gray Line approached the studio and was granted permission to have the buses tour past several of the most prominent back lot locations. Courthouse Square, the Tower of London, Colonial Square and the famous western streets area were all included in the tour, with the guide in the bus telling passengers all about the use of façades and special effects and pointing out movie stars when they presented themselves. Even though at this time there were no attractions, it became one of Gray Lines' most sought-after tours.

When MCA took over the studio in 1959, it continued the contract with Gray Line Tours, but by the early 1960s, Albert Dorskind—head of MCA/

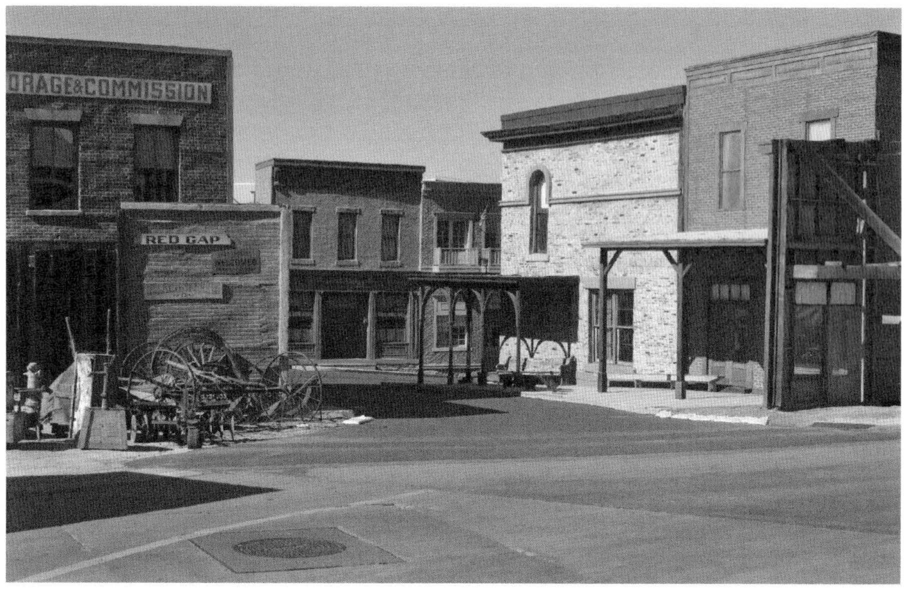

The famous "Five Points" western street location is still a part of the tram tour today.

Universal—in an effort to boost sales at the commissary and taking a lesson from Carl Laemmle, had asked Gray Line to stop at the commissary to allow tour guests to refresh themselves before continuing along the tour route. In 1962, Gray Line expanded this by providing a special tour called Dine with the Stars under the banner of Review Studio Tours. This became a very popular addition and paved the way for Universal taking over the tours.

Dorskind always knew that running the tours of the back lot in-house would be more profitable than leasing it to an outside vendor, so in 1964, he allocated $4 million to designing trams (which he thought would be quieter and more suited to the back lot than buses), building food courts and parking lots, installing restrooms and adding more things to do for paying guests. A makeup demonstration, an exhibit showcasing the costumes of Edith Head, a walk-through of Doris Day's dressing room and a Wild West shoot out were included. There was even one of Universal's famous monsters that could be made to "scare" guests with the push of a button. All of this for the low price of $2.50 for adults and $1.50 for kids. As the actual date of the opening of the new tour has been lost to time, Universal claims it to be June 17, 1964.

The tour in those early days was ninety minutes roaming through the back lot with a stop off at the commissary. The new attractions were mainly set up in the basement, so once the guests were finished with lunch, they would head downstairs and continue their day. Later, Prop Plaza opened as a midway stopover. Here, guests could view various movie props as well as the studio's first animated attraction, a Ford Model T attached to a moving scene that made it seem like the car was traveling down the road. Prop Plaza also was the site of the first Wild West Stunt Show. More and more people were hearing about the new tour, and the studio was having trouble keeping up with the growing crowds. In an effort to expand, Dorskind made a deal with Caltrans (state road works) to remove the top of the large hill in exchange for the usable dirt for the construction of the new Hollywood Freeway. In 1967, the Universal Tour Entertainment Center opened on the upper lot and became the start of the amusement park that we know today.

From 1967 on, the studio tour grew steadily. The Universal Amphitheater opened and became a premier concert and show location; more attractions and shows were added. Universal was determined to make the studio a location where a family could come and spend an entire day exploring and spending money within the park. Creative designers set about developing new and exciting attractions for the tour, and some of the early additions were the Parting of the Red Sea, the Collapsing Bridge and the Flash Flood. All of these are still present within the back lot if not always in use, but their continued presence is a testament to the team's ingenuity and the builders' prowess. Now, along with guests being able to view actual movie sets and locations like the Bates Motel and the Psycho House, they were treated to real-life special effects.

One of the things that has always made Universal's in-house tour so much more complete than the old Gray Line or bus tours was the tour guides themselves. Universal likes to call the guides Ambassadors to Hollywood, and there is no shortage of young up-and-comers who want the job. These guides are no slouches; they must go through a grueling three-week training course of tests designed to gauge their communication and improv skills, knowledge of current affairs and media savvy. They have to study and learn from a 250 plus–page guide manual, which they will be tested on and must pass before they will be hired on a permanent basis. In essence, the guides are entertainers, and since they never know what type of filming schedule will alter the tour route, they must be prepared at a moment's notice to adapt to the change seamlessly so the guests are none the wiser. Many of today's Hollywood stars got their start as Universal tour guides: *Saturday Night Fever* director John Badham, former Walt Disney Company chairman Michael Ovitz, singer Jack Wagner and

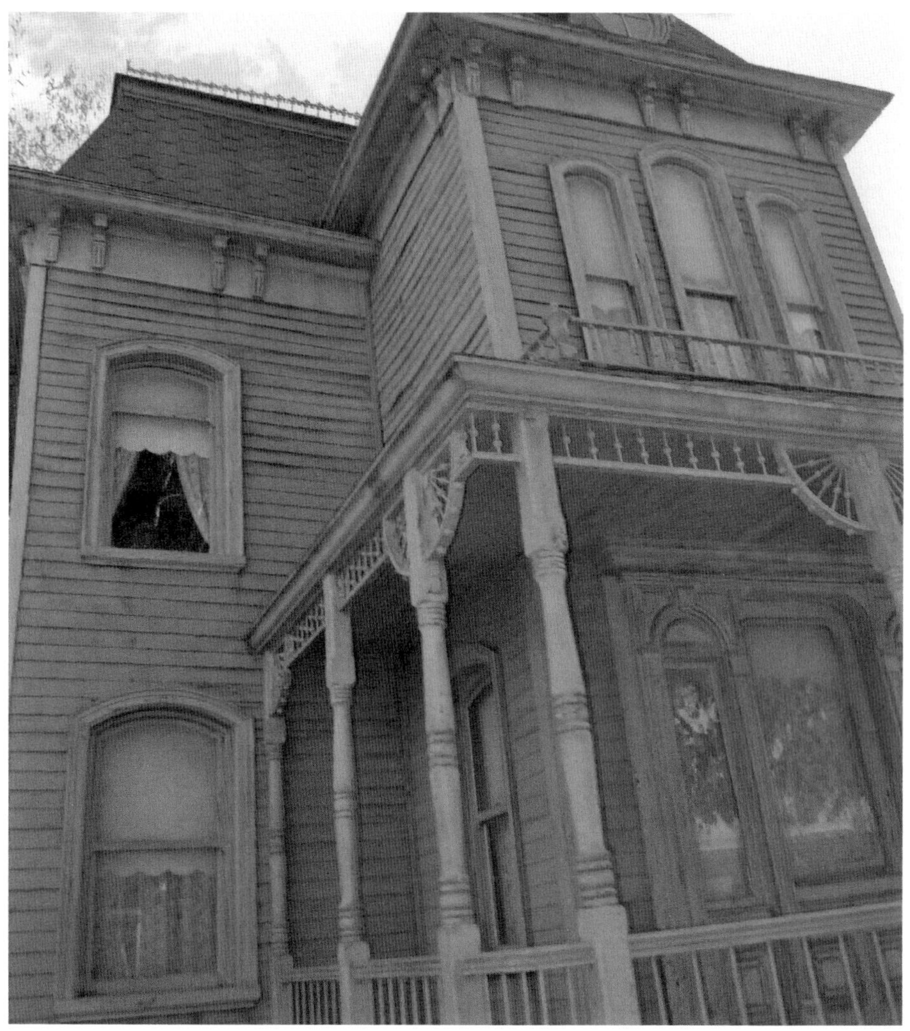

While on the Glamour Tram, look closely while passing Mother's House. You may just see her staring from the window.

actor/comedian Jimmy Fallon, to name just a few. Fallon now stars on the tour with his permanent role as a video host.

Another major draw of the tour is the possibility of guests seeing their favorite movie stars making an appearance, as the tram travels past movie sets. Doris Day, Lucille Ball, Alfred Hitchcock and any number of Hollywood celebrities have been spotted while traveling the back lot. On one occasion, John Travolta was leaving the studio grounds and his Rolls-Royce almost collided with one of the trams. Travolta, always one to be kind to people, held up the tram and made sure to meet and have his picture taken with as many of the guests as approached him. One time—a surprise for not only the guests but the tour driver and guide as well—Jim Carrey dressed up as Norman Bates and menaced guests with a rubber knife as they passed the Psycho House and motel. His actions were so well received that Universal made the "attack" a permanent part of the tour.

In 1976, what would eventually become the signature attraction for Universal Studios opened, and the Jaws Experience became one of the most popular sights on the tour route. Guests see a fully functioning twenty-five-foot animatronic shark attack their tram, and they can view the original Bruce the Shark prop from the movie *Jaws* displayed on the upper lot. More animatronic and special effects attractions were added over the years—some successful, others not so much—and even though the crowds remained relatively steady, Universal had not broken through the bubble that would propel it to the level of chief amusement park rivals Disneyland and Knott's Berry Farm. The leaderships was keenly aware that the studio/attraction had become surrounded by amusement parks, with Six Flags Magic Mountain nearby to the north.

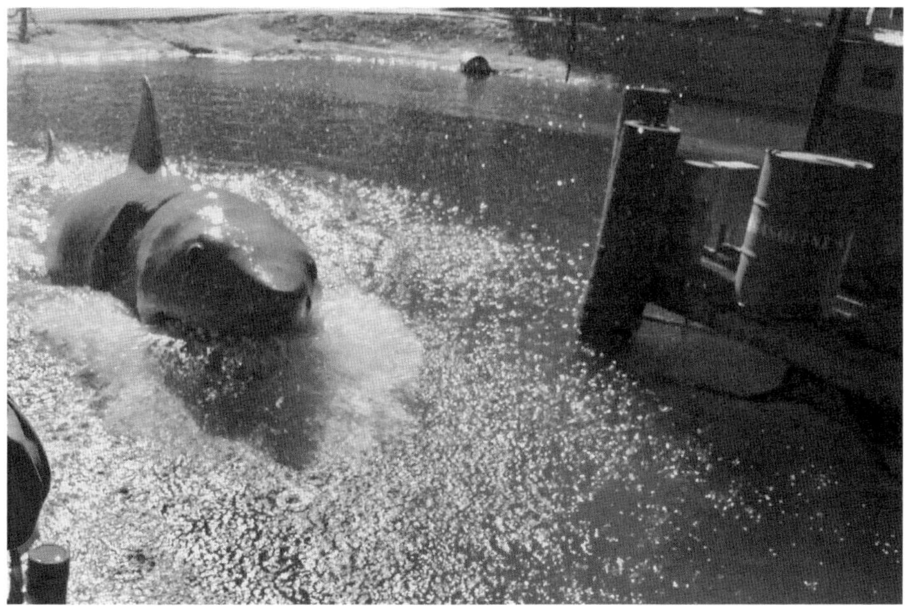

Bruce the Shark from the movie *Jaws* still plies the waters of Amity Island trying to eat tour guests if they get too close.

Universal knew that to try to compete with the other amusement parks on the same level and with the same model wouldn't be feasible; after all, Universal studios was still an active movie studio and would always remain so. Executives decided that the best way for Universal to become equal to the competition was to just be themselves. As one of the most well-known studios in Hollywood, why not capitalize on the movies? In the way that the films brought more excitement to the tour, they could also do the same for the rest of the property.

With the studio tour remaining the signature attraction, the park began to grow, adding even more to the famous back lot, with additions such as the Ice Tunnel and the Avalanche as well as the Battle of Galactica. Once the guests stepped off the Glamour Trams, they were treated to spectacular special effects–heavy shows like the Castle Dracula, the A-Team and the Adventures of Conan: Sword and Sorcery. More eateries were added, and the Universal Amphitheater was upgraded and expanded. Other additions to the after-tour area were a replica of KITT from the *Knight Rider* TV show (the car was set up so you could ask questions of KITT and receive answers), as well as numerous shopping opportunities. In the late 1980s, perhaps one of the most cherished attractions was added to the tour when King Kong opened. Earthquake—The Big One was added and a multimillion-dollar expansion undertaken on the lower lot, which is accessible by a quarter-mile-long escalator descending from the upper lot. Then, in June 1991, Universal's first standalone ride opened when the ET Adventure debuted. Over the following years, new attractions were added, and old attractions and rides disappeared and were replaced by more current movie-themed draws. Then there are those attractions that are no longer present due to circumstances beyond the control of Universal. This is what happened to the beloved King Kong animatronic.

Universal Studios' placement in the wooded hills behind Hollywood created a challenge for designing sets and also made it a magnet for fire dangers. Over the years, many such fires caused destruction and heartache for the studio, beginning as early as 1932. In that year, fire burned fifty acres, four movie sets and a steamship, all of which cost Universal just over $100,000. The year 1949 saw another blaze erupt; in 1957, the back lot lost a section of the famous New York Street to fire; and 1967 saw another devastating conflagration when the area of Little Europe, Denver, Laramie and European Streets were all destroyed. This fire cost the studio $1 million and sent flames leaping two hundred to three hundred feet into the air. Fires again erupted in 1987, 1990 and 1997. The first two of these fires turned out to be deliberately set, and although arson was also suspected in the 1997 fire, it turned out to be a chemical source rather than deliberate. These last three fires, as destructive as they were, didn't even come close to the loss suffered in the last big blaze to take place at Universal's back lot.

In 2008, while workers used a blow torch to apply asphalt shingles to a backdrop, they inadvertently ignited a flame that went unnoticed for almost two hours. By the time a security guard saw the fire and the studio fire crew arrived, the blaze was already getting out of hand, and additional fire services were called. The efforts to quell the fire were hampered by unusually low water pressure, and it took over seventeen hours to extinguish the blaze. New York Street and New England Streets were completely destroyed, and at least two sides of Courthouse Square had burned down, but the famous Courthouse itself was spared. This is the fire that also destroyed the King Kong attraction, which devastated many frequent guests to the studio. What made this fire so destructive, however, wasn't the sets or the tour attraction that had been destroyed but that it had spread to the nearby film vault. When the news of the vaults loss hit the airwaves, a cry was heard around the world. People were demanding to know how something so devastating could have happened. It was reported that the vault in question was where the studio kept its copies of its films and not the originals. The news that none of the actual films had been lost caused a sigh of relief to be had by all. Universal's copy of Robin Williams's film *What Dreams May Come* was lost, but a worldwide search turned up another copy, which was obtained from Europe.

King Kong was finally rebuilt, but the beloved animatronic puppet was gone. In its place was a new and exciting 3D attraction that was sure to thrill the guests as Kong saves the tram from rampaging dinosaurs. With Jurassic Park: The Ride, Revenge of the Mummy, along with The Simpsons ride and Despicable Me: Minion Mayhem, 3D coaster simulators, as well as numerous other rides, spectacular shows and family entertainment, Universal put itself on equal footing with its rivals Disney and Knott's. When Universal CityWalk opened in 1993, Universal seemed to complete its plan for an all-encompassing, all-day (and now all-night) entertainment venue. Once CityWalk was refurbished, its cinema redone and additional stores and upscale eateries were added, even Disney took notice and built the Downtown Disney area in conjunction with its new California Adventures theme park.

Knott's Berry Farm may be the progenitor of Halloween Horror events, but Universal Studios has arguably become the one to attend. After all,

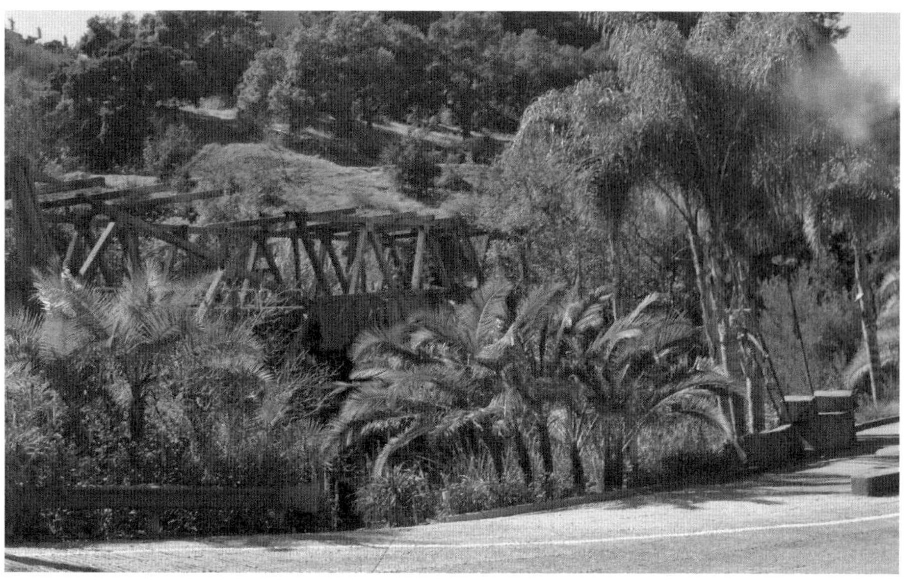

The collapsing bridge, although no longer used on the tour, has survived modernization and fires and can still be seen today.

who better to create the scariest, most diabolical Halloween monsters than Hollywood makeup artists employed by the very studio that created some of the most iconic and frightening monsters of all time? Horror events started at Universal Hollywood in 1986, but it was Universal Florida that actually launched Fright Nights in 1991; the name was changed to Halloween Horror Nights in 1992, the same year Universal Hollywood held its first event, and the name has remained ever since. The event was not held again in Hollywood until 1997 and then only for three years. It wasn't until 2006 that it became a permanent, monthlong attraction that is still going to this day, albeit much bigger and better than ever. In connection with the growing Halloween event, the studio added a nighttime back lot tour to the existing schedule, and it has become a favorite with many guests. This special tram tour is often approached by many from Universal's famous monster pantheon, much to the delight of guests. It was during the research phase for this night tour that producers discovered one of the many spirits that lingers on at the studio even to this day. Add in the new Wizarding World of Harry Potter–themed area, and you have the recipe for success unrivaled by any other park.

Universal Studios has stood the test of time. From its not so humble beginnings, through the war years, the lean times and devastating fires, this heart and soul of Hollywood has come out on top time and time again. Now, in the twenty-first century, Universal is poised to become one of, if not the premier amusement venue in the world. With two parks in Florida combined into one resort, another park in Japan and one in Singapore, Universal has started its takeover of the world amusement stage. Plans are already in the works for parks in Beijing and Moscow, and if they are successful, who knows where else they may build. One thing, however, must always be remembered. Universal Studios Hollywood is still the original, still the only one of its properties where guests can board the Glamour Tram and see actual, working movie sets both new and old. It is also the only amusement park where guests can see their favorite movie stars just being themselves while at work. Universal Studios is still in an amusement class of its own and hopefully will remain as such for a very long time.

7
Ghosts of the Back Lot

The Universal back lot is not only home to some of the most famous TV and movie set locations in history—nor is it just the route for the famous Glamour Tram Tour—it also is home to some spirits, both famous and obscure, that for whatever reason have felt that it was not quite time for them to pass on. Most people aren't aware that these spirits are lingering on the studio grounds, while a select few are quite well remembered. Whether you are one of those who are familiar with these tales or a novice to the Universal ghosts, it's time to get better acquainted with the ghosts of the back lot.

Up, Up and...Away?

When Universal City held its grand opening in March 1915, it had been planned that famed aviator Frank Stites would wow the gathered audience with a feat of harrowing aerobatics. Stites was scheduled to perform these stunts on opening day, but the wind through the mountain passes that surrounded Universal City began gusting so heavily that Stites's performance was postponed until the following day. Stites helped make the decision; just that morning, Frank had gotten word that his friend and rival Lincoln Beachey had been killed two days earlier while performing a stunt over the San Francisco Bay.

The second day of the opening day events dawned just a bit overcast, and Stites prepared for the upcoming stunt. Gone were the heavy gusts of the day before, and Frank lifted off the ground as planned and on time. The stunt, however, went every way but as planned, and when Frank Stites's body hit the ground after he jumped from his stricken airplane, "his spinal column was driven into his skull," according to the *Los Angeles Times*. Stites, who was poised to become "the world's greatest aviator," was dead at the young age of thirty-two.

Frank was all but forgotten over time, just another footnote in the history of the famed studio. No one seemed to care or even think about him within the movie industry or at Universal—that is, until the summer of 2015. That year, the creative director for the ever-popular Halloween Horror Nights was given the job of bringing the attraction back to the studio after it had been on hold for the last five years. One of the things that the creative director wanted to start up was a new, nighttime back lot tour to be offered with a paid Halloween event ticket. This Terror Tram, as it was going to be called, would travel around the established tour route but with monstrous interruptions.

One night, while he and his assistant were roaming around the area near the Psycho House, he heard the sound of giggling. The director knew that he and his assistant were the only ones in that section of the back lot, and even though the giggle only lasted a moment, the "diabolical" tenor of the sound frightened him to the point of fleeing. His assistant had to convince the director to come back, which took a while, but then, just as he returned, the giggling sounded again but this time much closer. Both he and his assistant fled from the area, and neither returned that evening.

The following day, the news of the director and his aide had already made its way around the staff room before he had even made it to work. Needless to say, most of the staff found it quite amusing that a man who had a deep love for all things horror and who had been a "haunter" for most of his life had been so easily frightened by a ghost. There were those that just assumed that the two had come across a security guard who had either inadvertently scared the two Horror Nights staff members or had decided to play a joke on them. Whichever was the case, it made it even more amusing for those who didn't believe in spirits. There were others, however, who decided that, since their boss had an experience, they would open up about strange events that had happened to them on the back lot as well. Many of the things the director was being told were markedly different from what had happened to him the night before. There was one story repeated by several staff members, and though some of the details were different, the story and sightings were all the same.

Quite a few people told him that they saw a figure wearing a vintage pilot uniform replete with an old-fashioned leather flight helmet wandering around as if dazed in the same location that he had heard the giggling the night before. This got the director to thinking, so he began to ask other employees about this lone figure; it turned out this person had been seen for many, many years in the area, and all of the stories were the same. Thinking that this was possibly an actual spirit lurking in the back lot, the director began to research any deaths that might have taken place during filming of movies that had an aviation theme to them. He figured the ghost must have been an actor or extra who had passed away during filming. Although he did not find any evidence of a film mishap in the studio archives, he did come across an old *Los Angeles Times* article dated March 17, 1915, that talked about the opening days of Universal City.

The article that the Halloween Horror Nights director found had lines and lines of mundane news regarding opening weekend, but one section caught his eye: the tale of the sad ending of Frank Stites. It identified the location of his death as being the same area where he and his assistant had heard the giggling and the same location that all of the other employees claimed to have seen the phantom aviator roaming about. Could the spirit of the back lot actually be Frank Stites's ghost? The director did a search for Stites to gather more information about the man, and although he did find plenty of stories regarding Stites's life, he realized that after the aviator's death, Frank had simply vanished from the papers. Air pioneers who continued to make a name for themselves had completely forgotten about all of his accomplishments and contributions to the advancement of aviation. Could Stites be wandering the back lot with the hope that he would be remembered? Perhaps he thought that if his ghost were seen his memory would linger as well?

Wondering if the spirit of Frank Stites was hanging out in the back lot of the studio for recognition had given the director an idea. He went to the prop department and grabbed a mannequin, went over to wardrobe and, from the discards section, gathered up enough pieces of costume to create a passable version of a 1910s-style aviator's outfit. Once his creation was complete, the director took the effigy to the area where the activity was reported and placed it as close as possible to the spot where Frank Stites died. After the mannequin was in position, the director spoke a few words to Stites, letting him know that he was and would be remembered. Since the effigy has been in place, no more giggling has been heard, and the specter of Frank Stites hasn't been seen since—well, mostly.

Halloween Horror Nights is now a yearly event, and because of this, many people are involved in making it the premier haunting event in Southern California. Because of this, it is almost never the same set designers and set grips that work the same area each year. One year, not realizing what the mannequin's purpose was and thinking it was just a minor back lot set piece, someone repurposed the tribute as a monster during the studio's Halloween haunt. During that year's event, many guests asked about the actor who was dressed as an old-time pilot, and many wondered just how the studio had made him look transparent and how he was able to pass through seemingly solid objects. Being that Universal is one of the greatest movie studios in existence, most guests just assumed it was a special effects trick and didn't give it a second thought—the employees who worked that area, however, knew there was something odd afoot.

Many of the scare actors working in the area of the Psycho House that year began to notice strange shadows passing near them. They would see them out of the corners of their eyes, but when they would look directly at the spot where they thought the figure to be, nothing was there. Others saw

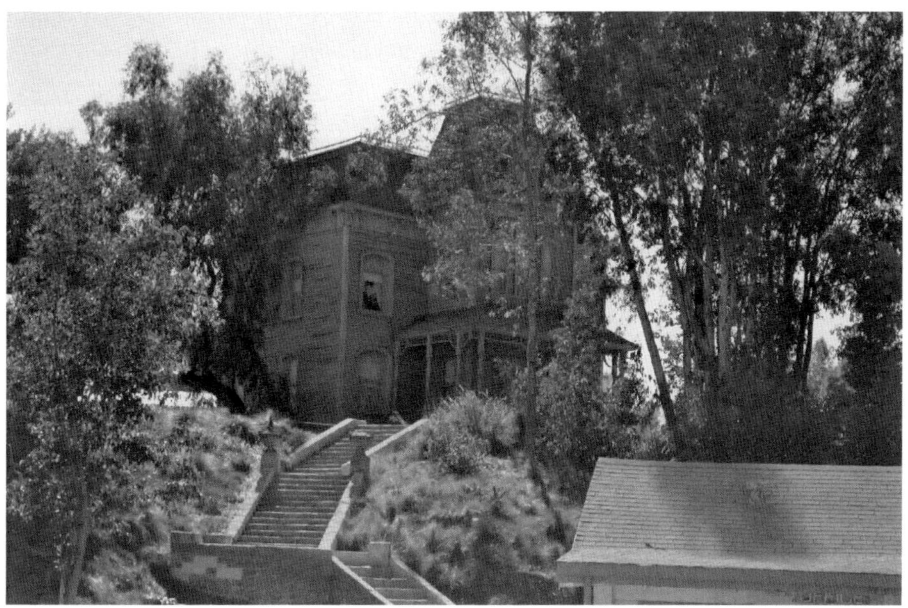

The Bates House from the movie *Psycho* has become one of the most recognizable homes in the world.

this shadow figure and heard giggling, just as the director and his assistant had; some heard grunts and thuds as if something had fallen on or near someone, and still others heard their names faintly called out, as if someone were luring them. If the scare actors heeded the voice and followed to where it beckoned, there would be no one there when they arrived. Many of these actors asked to be relocated within the event, and a few actually quit rather than be placed back in that location.

The director who had originally discovered that the spirit was that of Frank Stites caught wind of what was happening and decided to go back to the spot where he had placed the mannequin to see what might be causing these new disturbances. He knew right away why the ghost had returned; someone had removed the effigy. The director quickly found out where the figure had been moved, located the pilot uniform and immediately had the likeness put back where it belonged. Once again, all was quiet on the back lot. It would seem that as long as the effigy of Frank Stites remains near where his body fell that fateful day in March 1915, his spirit is content in the thought that he is remembered; take his likeness away, and Frank wanders the back lot, perhaps in an attempt to scare the studio into making sure he is not forgotten. Whatever the case may be, when you are touring around the famous back lot on one of the bright Glamour Trams, keep an eye out for Frank and give him a wave if you spot his mannequin. Who knows, it might just be the man himself.

Having a Ball

No one really knows why a person lingers after death or why he or she stays in a certain place. There are spirits that remain behind in a place where they felt comfortable, and others are seen in more than one of the places they frequented in life. Lucille Ball is one of these wandering spirits, and one of the places she has been known to appear is none other than Universal Studios.

Lucy is perhaps the most famous comedienne who ever lived. Her sitcom *I Love Lucy*, which ran from 1951 to 1956, is still in syndication today, and one would be hard pressed to find a person who has not heard of the show, let alone watched as Lucy and her cohort Ethel Mertz get into all sorts of onscreen trouble. Lucy and Desi became such big Hollywood stars that they formed their own studio, Desilu, and became legends in a town of legends.

Lucy, for her part, also had a stellar movie career, starting with a string of uncredited roles beginning in 1927 and continuing until the day she retired. With well over one hundred movies and countless television appearances, along with hundreds of episodes from her three TV series, Lucille Ball could be classified as the most prolific actress/comedienne in the history of stage or cinema; maybe this is one of the reasons that Lucille Ball has remained in this realm after death and is seen in so many different places.

When I was a young boy, my mother used to take my sister and me to Universal Studios often. It was one of those places that was easy for her to drive to and an inexpensive way to spend a fun-filled day. One of the things I always remembered from these trips was when the Glamour Tram would let us off near the lower lot and allow us to venture through Lucy's bungalow/dressing room. Back then, I wasn't thinking about ghosts or hauntings, but I can recall one of the tour guides talking about some of the spirits that haunted the back lot. I wonder now if anyone would have thought that Lucy would return to her bungalow after her death? Lucy's dressing room was located right across the street from sound stage 24 where her sitcom *Here's Lucy* was filmed during its first two seasons and very near the former attraction Lucy, A Tribute. Some of the reports from her former bungalow include things being moved on their own and makeup, costumes and props disappearing only to turn up later somewhere else in the rooms or even in a building next door. There have even been one or two reports of people in the old dressing room seeing a red-haired woman watching them who will give them a kindly smile before fading from view. Many believe that the woman is Lucille Ball and that the harmless pranks around the bungalow are Lucy's way of letting everyone know that she is still around and her sense of humor is intact.

Universal Studios is not the only place Lucy's spirit is seen. In the early days, Desilu's headquarters was in the Hart Building on the lot of Paramount Studios in Hollywood. Once wholly owned by Lucille Ball, it is today one of the oldest buildings on the lot. Lucy, although divorced from Desi in 1960, never stopped loving him. Despite all of his cheating and drinking, the two remained close friends right up until the day Desi passed away in 1986. The last words Desi said to Lucy were "I love you too, honey. Good luck with your show." Lucy had always loved the time they spent together filming and once said it was the happiest time of her life. This may be the reason Lucy still hangs around the offices of the old Desilu studio.

Reports from those who work in the building say that a woman's ghost haunts the upper floor. They believe it is Lucy because the smell of Lucy's favorite perfume almost always precedes any activity. Many of the reports claim that objects are often tossed off of desks onto the floor by unseen hands; others claim that they have had things removed from their desk drawers or closets and have found them tossed on the floor in other offices down the hall. Quite a few of the reports are made by the male occupants of the building, and it is believed that Lucy, in her own impish way, is flirting with these men.

One of the more compelling stories from the Hart Building took place when a security guard was making the rounds of the floors and kept hearing the sound of doors opening and closing. The guard followed the noise as it moved, and when he finally caught up to the sounds, he watched as a door, seemingly of its own accord, slammed shut, reopened and then slammed shut once again. There was a report of a guard who had actually seen Lucy near her old office. The night watchman, not realizing that it may have been a ghost, approached a woman who was standing in the hallway to inquire about why she was in the building. When he was only a few steps away, the woman turned in his direction, smiled at the guard and simply vanished. The security guard, having grown up watching Lucy on TV, knew immediately who the woman was and that he had just seen Lucy's spirit.

The place that Lucy's spirit is most active is, of course, the house she lived in at the time of her death. On the night of April 17, 1989, Lucy started experiencing chest pains; her husband and daughter convinced her to go to the hospital, and she was immediately taken into an operating room, where she underwent seven hours of open-heart surgery. After she was sent home, she was told that she couldn't climb the stairs to her bedroom and was forced into the guest room. She was unable to care for herself, was being treated as an invalid and had been removed from the bedroom where she had lived with her first husband, Desi Arnaz, with whom she had bought the house. The day after Lucy arrived home, her surgically repaired aorta ruptured, and she was rushed back to the hospital; unfortunately, the doctors were unable to save Lucy this time, and she died on the operating table. Lucy's daughter said that her mother no longer thought life was worth living and had decided it was time to move on. With the many reports of activity from the owners who had bought the house after her passing, it is unlikely that Lucy actually did move on.

Gary Morton, Lucy's second husband, sold the house on Roxbury Drive a few years after Lucy passed. The new owners had the house demolished—although no one really knows why—and had a completely new home built. It would seem that Lucy was not happy with the changes. There is a report of one of Lucy's friends driving past her old home to get a last look at the house. While driving slowly by, the friend glanced up and noticed a woman standing in Lucy's old bedroom. The walls in the front of the house had already been torn down, and the friend had an unobstructed view and was shocked when she realized that it was Lucy she was seeing. As the passerby stopped her car, Lucy turned toward her and, with a confused and angry look, walked around a corner of the upstairs floor and vanished from view.

Once the new house was completed, the reports of activity continued. Many owners who have lived in the home since Lucy's death have claimed that furniture will rearrange while they are away from home, and items will move from one room to another, even while the owners are present. Boxes will be stacked in strange places or moved to different rooms. It would seem that quite a bit of the activity in the home takes place up in the attic. It is not uncommon for ghosts to reside in this part of any house as many paranormal investigators know, and Lucy has decided that she is comfortable there as well. Sounds have been heard at all hours of the day and night from the attic and range from the laughter and talking of a loud party to one owner claiming that the *I Love Lucy* theme would play through the vents of the attic throughout the house. Owners have heard the sounds of furniture and boxes stored in the attic moving around on their own and a woman's laugh at the confusion the noise brought. Even with all of the reports coming, they all claim that the activity is never threatening or overly scary, it is mainly playful and fun. It would seem that Lucille Ball just loves her old home and likes to hang around her old neighborhood.

THE PHANTOM AND THE SOUND STAGE

One of the most unique sound stages on the Universal lot also was one of the oldest. Sound stage 28 was originally built in 1925 for the filming of *The Phantom of the Opera*. The reason we say it was unique has to do with the fact that the entire Paris Opera House interior that we see on the screen was built directly into the stage walls. Over the many years that the sound stage was in use, this same opera house scene was used for various movies. Some of the other films shot in this studio include *Uncle Tom's Cabin*, *The Birds* and *The Sting*. Along with these films, a few of Universal's horror movies were filmed in stage 28: *Bride of Frankenstein*, *Dracula*, *Psycho* and the 1943 remake of *Phantom of the Opera*, which used the same built-in opera house set as the original film.

Sound stage 28 used to be a part of the back lot tram tour. For those who wanted to get a glimpse into the actual stage, Universal used to conduct VIP tours of the building, which allowed guests to get up close and personal with the famous opera house set and view some of the areas where the stars would get ready for their upcoming movie shoots. Many of those on these tours had heard about the supposed hauntings of the sound stage and would inquire about the stories while listening to the guides. Most wanted to know if it was true that Lon Chaney, the "Man of a Thousand Faces," was indeed still hanging around the set of his most famous movie.

Lon Chaney was born Leonidas Frank Chaney on April 1, 1883, to parents who were both born deaf. Lon needed to learn sign language to speak with his parents, and that—coupled with having to pantomime as well during conversations with them—gave Lon an uncanny ability at acting during the silent era of film. Chaney's brother owned a theater, so Lon began acting onstage at an early age, and by 1912, he was trying out for parts on the silver screen. He was usually cast in minor parts as a villain, and his first big break came in 1919, when he was cast as a cripple called "the Frog" in the film *The Miracle Man*. Another aspect of Lon Chaney's brilliance mentioned in an earlier chapter was his masterful use of makeup, which allowed him to portray any creature, human or monstrous. Lon Chaney truly was a complete actor, and I dare say no one has come close to his overall expertise.

Even though Lon Chaney had been acting for many years before his starring role in *The Phantom of the Opera*, it was this film that made him a star. His haunting portrayal of Erik, the hideously scarred monster of the film, scared the hell out of audiences and caused them to feel an odd sort of sympathy for the lovelorn character that they couldn't quite understand. Chaney, for his part, always had a deep appreciation for the way fans responded to his Erik, and he always thought that *Phantom* was one of his best roles. Could this affinity Lon Chaney had for his character and this movie be the reason that he stayed in the sound stage long after his death?

Over the years, those working in stage 28—or as it was known, the Phantom Stage—knew that it was haunted. The security guards who were tasked with patrolling the stage late at night knew this more than most. One of the first reports of activity came from a guard who was working late one night. As he was walking near the back of the stage where the Paris Opera House set was located, he heard a noise above him. When the

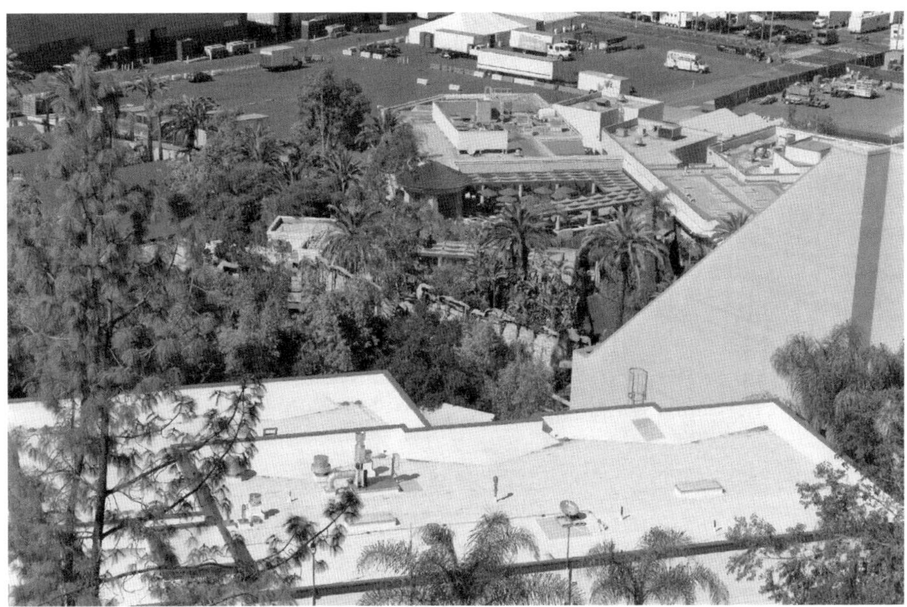

This part of the lower lot shows where the sound stages are located. You can see where stage 28 was located in the upper right corner behind the park now surrounded by fencing.

man looked up, he was surprised to see a caped figure staring down at him. When the guard called up to the figure that he needed to come down and get out of the building, the figure darted down the catwalk and vanished from view. The startled guard realized that as the man fled he made no sound whatsoever—no noise from the wooden walk, no sound from the metal railing and no sound of footsteps. The guard looked all around the stage but could find no sign of any intruder. When the guard told his superiors what had happened, they scoffed at him, but more reports were to follow.

Besides the continuing reports from the security guards, there have been many other studio employees who have seen the caped figure. Those stagehands who work on the catwalks have seen him many times. On those occasions, when a glimpse of the man's face has been seen, the description is always the same: it is the face of Lon Chaney. One of the strangest reports and one that has had numerous sightings is that of Chaney walking about the catwalks and outer areas of the studio carrying a chandelier. We find this report to be a bit farfetched, as the only chandelier that we know of that Lon Chaney would be attached to was the one used in the filming of his *Phantom* movie. The chandelier in question was forty feet in diameter and weighed approximately sixteen thousand pounds. It was an exact replica of the one in the Parisian opera house and was raised and lowered by a heavy chain. Why Chaney would be lugging this thing around is odd, but we can find no reports that it is a different light fixture. It is our assumption that what people are calling a chandelier is in actuality a candelabra. As all of the statements regarding these reports are very similar, we believe the tales have been repeated with wrong information.

Lon Chaney is not the only spirit who occupies the Phantom Stage. Sometime in 1925, during the filming of *Phantom of the Opera*, an electrician, working high up repairing a klieg light on the catwalks, lost his balance and fell to his death. Many visitors to the stage have reported seeing a man in old-fashioned clothing walking along the same catwalks as Chaney's spirit. The onlookers claim that the man is just going about his business as if he doesn't know he is dead and will oftentimes just disappear as they are looking at him. The lights within sound stage 28 seem to have a mind of their own and will often turn themselves off, sometimes during filming or other inopportune moments, then—as quickly and as mysteriously—will turn back on. Workers and guards who swear that they extinguished the lights when they left the stage for the evening will return in the morning or sometimes even days later to find that every light in the building has been turned back on. Many believe that this is the electrician having a bit of fun with the living.

The hit television series *Ghost Whisperer* used sound stage 28 often, and strange things would happen while filming. Odd shapes and figures would show up on film in the editing room, even when the crew knew that those figures weren't there during the shoot. Extreme cold spots would inexplicably happen around the actors while they were trying to perform their lines; sometimes these mysterious patches would be so cold that the actors would not be able to continue until the spot dissipated, and other times it would hit so suddenly that the actor would momentarily forget his or her lines and the scene would need to be reshot. There were times when lights would explode for no discernable reason and other times when the actors would actually see the cloaked and smiling figure of Lon Chaney in their dressing rooms. The crews who worked in the sound stage reported seeing Chaney in the prop room and in the rooms where costumes were stored. Guests and employees alike have heard the sound of doors opening and then closing and have witnessed doors slamming on their own as they passed by them.

In the almost one hundred years of service to the studio, sound stage 28 has seen two world wars, withstood the ravages of numerous earthquakes and destructive fires and weathered them all to stand proud on the back lot of Universal Studios. Unfortunately, as tourism has grown over the years and the demand for more and more attractions to please these fans has increased, the need for more rides and amusements has grown along with it. Universal Studios, being on a hillside and geographically limited on buildable land, has had to make space where possible. Sound stage 28's proximity to the theme park's lower lot section was a natural choice to be repurposed for the use of the tourist section of the studio and was slated for demolition.

Once word had gotten out about the stage's impending demise, a chorus of voices rose in an effort to have the stage and its opera house set declared a National Historic Landmark. Regrettably, neither the building nor the set qualified. Once historic status failed, a group of preservationists started a petition campaign to try to get Universal to reconsider its decision—this also failed. All was not lost, however.

Universal Pictures has always been very aware of the fragility of Hollywood history. It watched over the years as historic set after historic set was lost to the developer's whims. One of the worst cases of destruction came when MGM sold and allowed residential developers to tear down the sets for *Showboat*, *Tarzan* and some of the locations used in the filming of *Gone with the Wind* to erect tract homes. Universal was not about to make the same mistake.

The removal of sound stage 28 was a difficult decision for the studio. As it was built in 1925, the cost to make the stage completely soundproof—along with the needed upgrades to keep it competitive with the newer stages on the lot—made the investment more than the worth of the building. Universal began looking for museums and historic preservation groups that could take the opera set and display it to the public; this, too, was turning out to be a difficult task. As of this writing, Universal hasn't found anyone willing to take over the care of such an aged set piece, but the studio has not given up hope. Universal has carefully removed the Paris Opera House set—at least all of the original set pieces—and carefully warehoused them in a safe and protective environment. It is the hope of many that the studio can find someone who will show these museum pieces to the public; there also is talk of putting them on display at the theme park so future generations can see how Hollywood has evolved over the years.

Sound stage 28 may be gone, replaced by theme park entertainments and the smell of churros wafting through the air on a crisp summer evening. But what of the spirits who called the stage home? Have Lon Chaney and the phantom electrician finally moved on to their final rest, or have they just moved on to new digs within Universal? Could they now be entertaining guests in the lower lot of the amusement park area that was adjacent to the stage's location? The lower lot has many reports of paranormal activity, and who knows, maybe Chaney and our jokester electrician are a couple of the spirits now having fun with the guests in this area.

A HITCH IN HIS STEP

As a young man, Steven Spielberg used to sneak onto the Universal Studios lot and walk around dreaming of a time when he could enter without having to hide. Even though he wasn't supposed to be on studio grounds, no one ever stopped him because when they looked at him, clean cut and carrying a briefcase, they figured he belonged there. Spielberg knew that one day he would be part of Hollywood and Universal, and he never gave up that dream. One day, it came true.

Steven Spielberg is arguably the greatest director and producer to ever set foot in Hollywood, and his Amblin Entertainment group is now housed in the old bungalows that once were home to the stars of the past: Lucille Ball, Abbott and Costello, Tony Curtis and Alfred Hitchcock, one of the greatest directors in history and whose office Spielberg inherited, along with Hitchcock's ghost.

Shortly after Spielberg moved into his new offices, he began to notice strange things going on. He would hear noises while sitting at his desk as if someone had come up behind him. He would turn around to find an empty room. No matter the time of day or night, he would get the feeling that he was being watched. It was almost as if someone were looking over his shoulder. After a while, Spielberg started to realize that the most common answer to this feeling of not being alone was that there was a spirit present. Considering whose bungalow Spielberg was using and the fact that whoever it was liked to look over his shoulder while he worked on his film projects, he had a good idea who the spirit might be.

Spielberg began speaking to the spirit and calling it Alfred. He asked the spirit if he would kindly not bother him while working because the feeling the spirit gave him was unnerving. The ghost didn't scare him, but it made it hard for him to concentrate on his work. No matter how many times he asked Hitchcock to leave him alone, the dead director always ignored him.

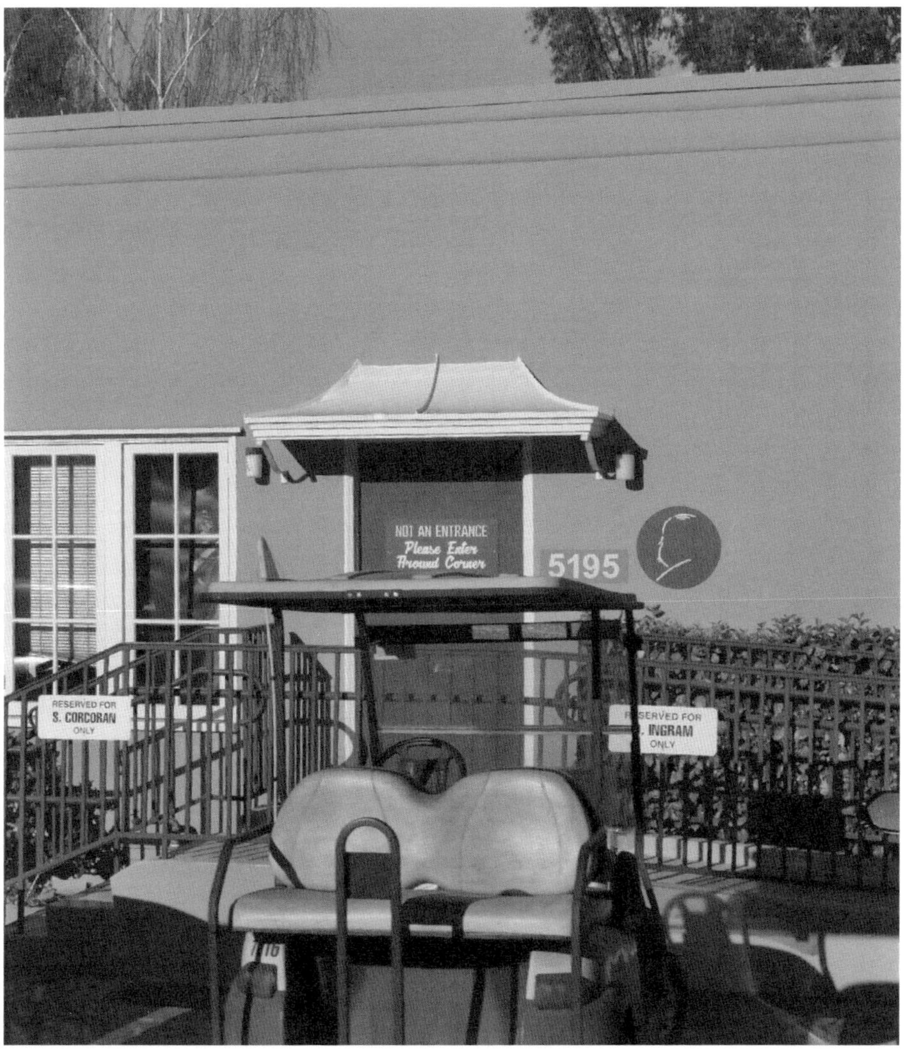

This bungalow belonged to Alfred Hitchcock both in life and in death as well as Steven Spielberg in his early days at Universal Studios.

Alfred Hitchcock always had a reputation for being difficult to work with, and now Spielberg could understand the reputation.

Over time, it became more and more difficult to get his work done in the office, and Spielberg was finally forced to find a new office. Amblin Entertainment is still housed in the old bungalows that Hitchcock used, but Spielberg's office is now away from the prying eyes of Mr. Hitchcock.

8
Ghosts of the Lower Lot

The lower lot area of Universal Studios opened to the public in March 1991 and was a much-anticipated addition to the theme park. It was named the Studio Center due to its location near many of the studio's original stages, dressing rooms and costume warehouses. This area is reached by a quarter-mile-long series of escalators called the Universal Stairway, which runs from the upper lot down to the new section. Some of the new attractions at the lower lot included World of Cinimagic, Lucy: A Tribute and, added in June of that same year, The E.T. Adventure. Today, this section of the park includes Revenge of the Mummy, an indoor roller coaster (which replaced the E.T. Adventure) and Transformers: The Ride, a thrilling dark ride. The jewel of the lower lot is one of the most expensive rides ever built and one that set new standards for ride theming and design, Jurassic Park: The Ride, an exhilarating adventure through Steven Spielberg's film world where riders get face-to-face with dinosaurs and get very wet. Another aspect of this area of Universal Studios is the large amount of haunting activity reported in this small section of the park.

Having spoken with many of the employees working in this section, it is clear that most believe this area is haunted. The Transformers ride is literally next door to where sound stage 28 was located, and Lucille Ball's dressing room is very near. With the moviemaking element of the studio directly behind the walls of the rides in this part of the theme park, it shouldn't come as a surprise that spirits might call it home.

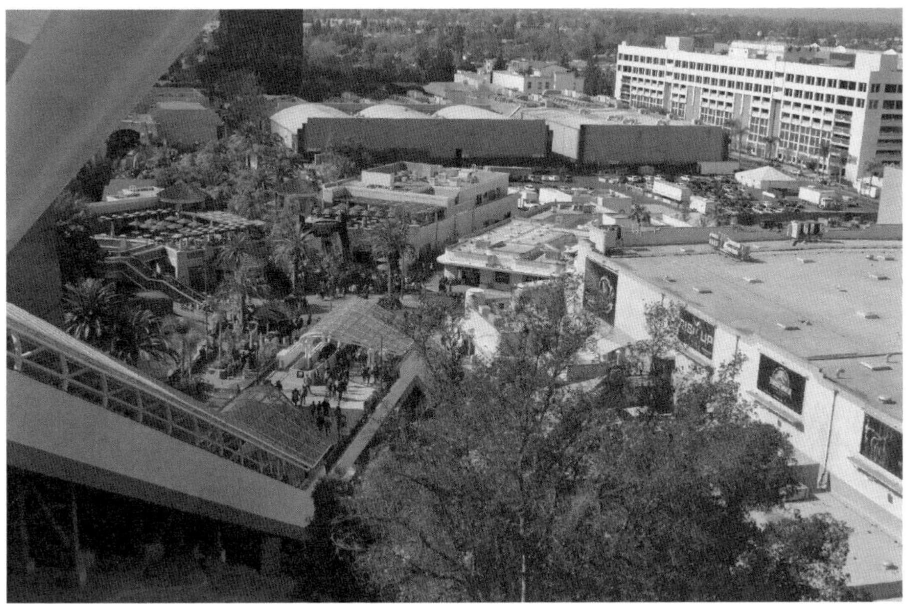

The lower lot section of the theme park as seen from the Universal Stairway.

I Want My Mummy

The lower lot at Universal Studios has some of the park's most thrilling rides. Transformers: The Ride, Jurassic Park: The Ride and, of course, Revenge of the Mummy. Jurassic is a wet ride where guests are menaced by lab-created dinosaurs, whereas Transformers is a three-dimensional special-effects dark ride. Revenge of the Mummy, however, is a thrilling indoor rollercoaster through the tomb of a long-dead pharaoh brought back to life as the evil mummy. The ride can be scary in and of itself...but when the riders catch a glimpse of the ghost that haunts the dark ride, it can become downright terrifying.

Reports of this spirit began coming in almost from the day the ride opened. Guests would come off of the roller coaster in a state of panic, having witnessed a young boy standing on the tracks as the car barreled down on him at forty-five miles an hour. At first, the employees would frantically shut down the ride and rush in, expecting to find an injured—or worse—deceased child lying on the platform. Every time the employees arrived at the area where the guests claimed to have seen the boy on the tracks, nothing could be found. There was no sign that anyone had been hit or had even been in the area. There also was nothing on the various security cameras set up within the ride.

The reports from the guests continued on and off for a few months following the opening of Revenge of the Mummy, but ride employees and supervisors were starting to see and hear things themselves. All of the reports from the roller coaster were the same. Riders in the front of the rollercoaster cars would spot what looked like a boy about ten years of age, wearing early twentieth-century clothing, standing on the tracks directly in front of their oncoming car. Just as the car was about to hit the child, he would turn, stare at the front seat passengers and wait as the car seemingly impacted his young body. The reports became a daily occurrence, and each and every time the ride operators were told about the young boy they would shut down the ride to make sure everything was OK. Even though they began to realize that what the guests were seeing on the rollercoaster was most likely a ghost, they still performed their due diligence of checking the ride for safety.

The reports began to fade after a few months, and it has been years since the child has been seen within the ride. However, as the reports became less frequent within the Revenge of the Mummy ride, the reports from the Ben & Jerry's (Studio Scoop) ice cream shop, which is part of the same building, have become more and more common. Could it be that this lost child has decided that ice cream is more to his taste?

No one knows who this lost little boy is, but the fact that he is always seen in old-fashioned clothing would indicate he was possibly a child actor who died playing a role. A more likely explanation might be that he had been living on and passed away at one of the many ranches that were bought up to create the studio. He may not realize he is dead, or perhaps he just enjoys all of the new sights and fun going on at the theme park and has decided to hang around. Whatever the case may be, it would be nice to find out who this young man is and possibly help him to move on into the afterlife.

FREEZER FIASCO

One of the security guards working in the lower lot had mentioned that the Ben & Jerry's (now Studio Scoop) ice cream shop had some "strange things" happen in and around the freezer. He said that some of the shop employees had called him over and asked him to check and see if a guest had snuck into the store because they kept hearing things moving around in the back. The guard went into the area where the freezer is located but couldn't find anything wrong. As he was leaving the area, however, he heard a noise behind him. When he turned back. he saw that the freezer door was open. Being a logical individual, the guard figured that the door had been only partially shut and had popped open due to his footsteps or some other vibrations. The guard closed the door and again turned to go, this time sure that the freezer door was securely closed. As the employee reached the entryway to the back room, he once more heard a noise behind him and noticed that the freezer door was open. This time, when he went to close the freezer, he checked to make sure there was nothing keeping the door from closing completely and even tried to pull the door open without using the latch handle. Once he knew that the freezer was as shut as it was going to be, he made to leave. Before he could even get completely turned, the door flew open and almost hit him in the back. The startled guard faced the freezer door, and as he watched, it slammed forcefully closed. The guard bolted for the exit.

After we heard this tale, we asked around at the Ben & Jerry's (Studio Scoop), but most of the employees were apprehensive to say anything.

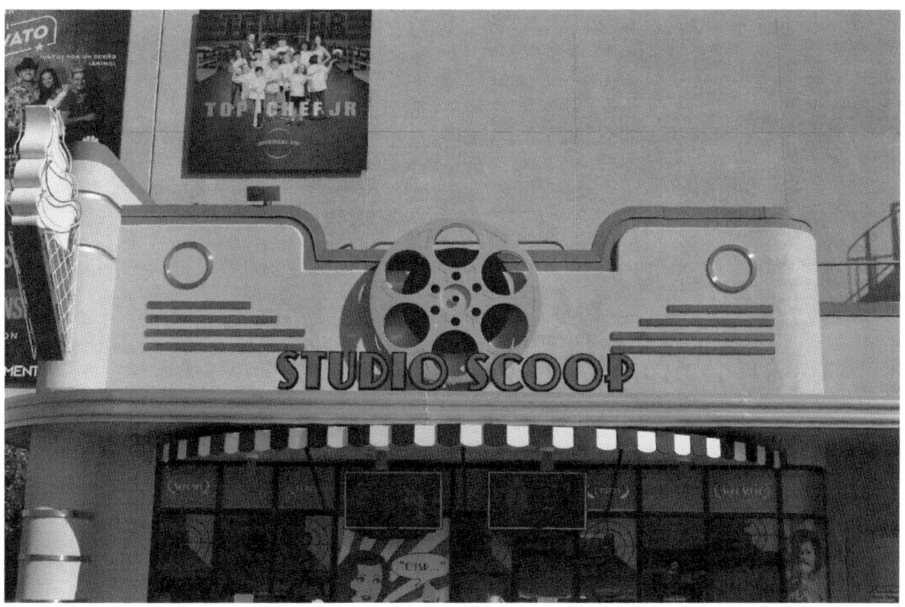

The Studio Scoop (formerly Ben & Jerry's) is where a spirit haunts the freezer.

There was one who mentioned that every now and again when they would walk into the freezer to get stock for the front ice cream freezer they would find that the ice cream containers would be moved from where they were supposed to be and even on a few occasions would find the freezer a mess. Some containers would be strewn around the shelves, while others would be on the floor. It was almost as if someone had gotten upset and thrown a tantrum inside the freezer box.

An Amazing Occurrence

Halloween Horror Nights is arguably the best Halloween haunt in California and perhaps the country. Every year, hundreds of hopeful scare actors try out to be part of the fun and frights, but only those with superb talent for the art of the scare make it onto the studio grounds to become part of Universal's historic frights. Maybe it is the pride people feel when they are accepted into the family at Universal or perhaps the knowledge that the world-class studio makeup artists are the ones who will be turning them into unrivaled monsters, but whatever it is that elicits the pride these scare actors feel about working the Halloween Horror Nights, at least one of them has decided that the show must go on even after his death.

The mazes that Universal sets up for the Halloween event are spread wide over the theme park and back lot of the studio. One of these mazes is usually put up on the lower lot right next to the Revenge of the Mummy ride and the Universal Stairways lower tier. It is this maze that one of the past scare actors has decided to return to each year to scare not only the guests who flock to this event but also those who are working hard themselves to scare the guests.

No one could tell me when the first time this spirit was seen, but over time, he has become common enough that those in the know consider him just a part of the show. One employee we spoke with told us that he is not limited to just one area of the maze but wanders around wherever he feels he is needed. One of the first times he was seen, another scare actor was stationed near the end of the maze and was wondering why he kept seeing another actor in his area when he thought he was alone in his section. He was not able to leave his post to find out who his cohort was but was almost in awe of this other person's ability to elicit screams from the guests as they walked past his hiding place. When the evening of work was over, the scare actor noticed his partner just standing out in the maze walkway and made his way over to introduce himself. As he approached, however, the other actor just turned, smiled and began walking away while fading into nothingness. There have been numerous reports from guests going through this maze of an actor vanishing from their sight. The guests will emerge from the attraction and ask how the special effect was done, as they were so close and yet could see no way the trickery could have been accomplished. At first, the employees had no idea what the tourists were talking about, but now they just smile and tell the confused guests that they are not allowed to divulge the secrets of the trade.

This actor apparently rests during the rest of the year, as there aren't any reports of his presence outside of the Halloween Horror Nights maze. No one is sure who this person is, how or why he died, but it is assumed that he was one of the first scare actors to participate in this maze when it was new. Hopefully, someday this devoted actor will be identified and given the recognition he deserves.

A Scary Character

The lower lot is the smallest section of the Universal theme park universe. Even if you include the disconnected Studio Tour Center, it is much smaller than either the back lot or the upper lot. Even though it is small in acreage, it is big in paranormal activity.

One place where activity occurs is the small souvenir Character Store (now called the Lower Lot Studio Store) sandwiched between the Studio Commissary (not the original) and the entrance to Jurassic Park: The Ride. When we asked around about any type of paranormal activity, many of the employees were reluctant to say anything. "I have only worked here for a month, go ask so and so," "Maybe you should ask our manager" or even the curt "No…no…no idea." It was on our third or fourth trip to the park that we finally got someone to answer. This employee asked that we not identify them but that they had a few experiences in the store, mostly at night and at times when the store was trying to open up for the day.

This person said that they were trying to help a customer one evening and that the customer was being a bit difficult. It seems the patron was looking for something that the store didn't carry but another store on the upper lot did. This employee tried to be patient, but it was becoming difficult, as the

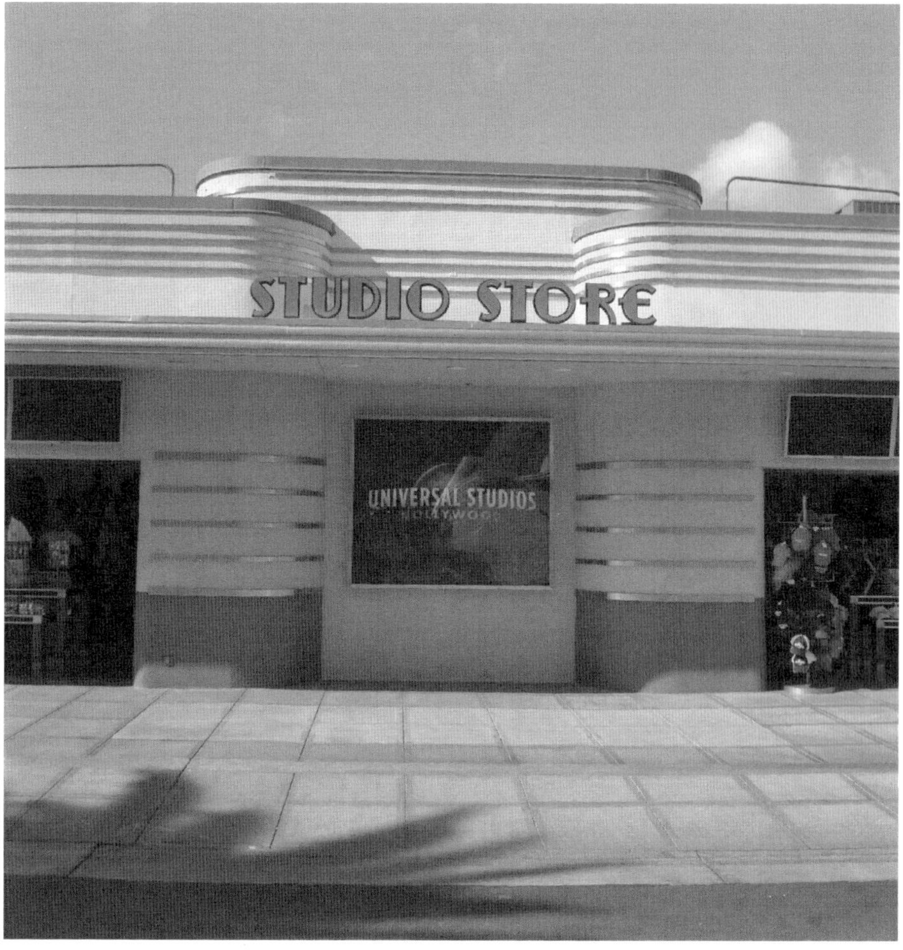

The Lower Lot Studio Store (formerly the Character Store) is where strange things occur without warning.

customer wanted the store employee to "run up and get them one." The store clerk related that they were about to say something to the customer when a stuffed doll hit the guest in the back of the head. Both the clerk and the customer turned to see who had hit the guest when another doll flew off the shelf and hit the customer directly in the face. The customer promptly left the store.

There are other times after the crowds have left and the store employees are closing up for the night that the lights will begin to turn off and on of their own accord and things will begin to simply fall off the shelves. When the employees open the shop up in the morning, they will find that things that had been on the shelves are now on the floor and other items have been moved from one display to another—sometimes things have been moved clear across the store to the opposite side.

There is some speculation that the spirit is the same little girl who haunts the Jurassic Outfitters store nearby. No one has ever seen her here, or any other spirit for that matter, but the playful nature of the pranks and the way the spirit will toss items at customers and employees alike if they get out of line seems childlike. Who this spirit is may never be fully known but has become just another part of the store.

OUTFITTED FOR FRIGHT

Perhaps the most haunted place in the lower lot is the Jurassic Outfitters store directly adjacent to the Jurassic Park: The Ride attraction. People exiting the ride itself are channeled through this shop and greeted with all sorts of merchandise related to the ride and the blockbuster movies from which it is derived. The riders usually stop to browse the wares, and most are oblivious to the fact that there is a very active spirit in their midst, one who is not shy about letting people know she is there.

No matter how many times we stop in to talk with the employees at Jurassic Outfitters, almost all of them have a ghost story to tell. Many of these tales are similar to those told to us at the Character Shop: things being moved around in the middle of the night, items mysteriously falling off the shelves for no discernable reason and lights that flicker on and off of their own accord. There are a couple of things here that go far beyond the reports from the other shop.

One thing that is different here at Jurassic Outfitters is that the spirit of a little girl has actually been seen in the store. One employee told us that she had been working near the end of the day and was looking forward to closing up shop. There were only a few patrons left, and they appeared to be just browsing, when she noticed a little girl wandering around in the area where some small toys were sold. This little girl looked between eight and ten years old and seemed like she might be lost. The store employee watched the girl for a couple of minutes, and when she realized that there was no adult with the child, she slowly approached her. As the store clerk got near to the little girl, the child turned toward her, stared and then simply shook her head and disappeared from sight. The employee said she was shocked at what she had just seen but remembered her co-workers telling her that the store was most likely haunted. That had just been confirmed for her in a most convincing way.

This type of occurrence with the little girl seems to be very common in Jurassic Outfitters, as we have heard quite a few variations of it while talking to the employees at the store. There was one tale told to us that varied from the rest, and it sounded like it could have been right out of one of Universal's famous horror movies.

A store clerk told us that she was working one evening around dusk and that the crowd was light but constant. She was standing at the register near the exit to the lower lot area and was watching the guests as they browsed the various items for sale in the shop. She said that as she turned to look outside the store, a mist began to form right near the entrance. She said that the mist came out of nowhere and that there was no fog that night and no special effects going on that would cause it either. As she watched, the mist became so thick that it completely obscured the view of everything beyond the doorway. The clerk went on to say that the mist started to creep into the store, and the guests began to notice and stare at it as well. The strange fog came into the store about ten feet and stopped. Now the customers began to back away, some of them commenting that it had to be part of the Jurassic ride, some malfunction of the dry ice fog machine or something similar. The

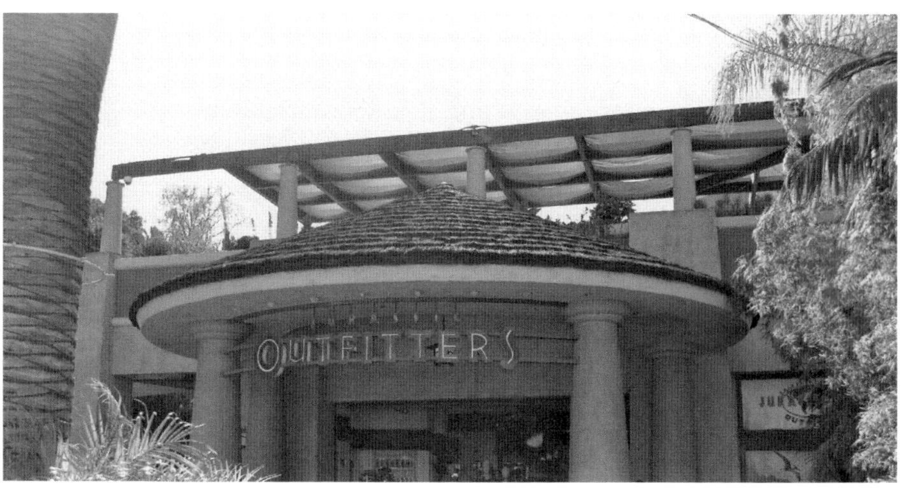

A little girl is believed to haunt this shop on the lower lot.

clerk told us that any type of special effect apparatus would be isolated to the inside of the ride structure. Universal prides itself on its safety record and would not have any machinery of this type in proximity to the park guests.

The crowd of onlookers was beginning to move toward the exit, having become bored with the wayward fog, and just as they began to step forward, the mist began to dissipate. Just as the fog was about to completely disappear, the clerk heard a sharp giggle, and all of the merchandise near where the mist had been flew off the shelves and landed on the floor among the startled guests' feet. This event took place near the Halloween season, and even though Halloween Horror Nights had not yet begun, the guests began to applaud as if they had just watched a show. The clerk figured that they assumed it was just another of Universal Studios' famed special effects shows geared toward the opening of the scare season. The employee, however, knew better.

Stairway to Heaven?

There is one other tale involving the lower lot, and we have heard from two employees about it. It seems to be a fairly rare occurrence, but because we did hear about it, we are including the story.

While we were talking with one of the security guards on a trip to the park, he mentioned that while patrolling the lower lot well after closing, he noticed that someone was riding on the bottom section of the Universal Stairway (the three-tier escalator that connects the lower lot with the upper lot of the amusement park). He told us that he had just come out from the office across the way and was surprised that there would be anyone in the area other than another guard. He knew there were no night film shoots nearby, so this section of the park should have been empty.

The guard walked over to where he had seen the figure on the escalator, but when he arrived at the spot, he couldn't see the person anymore. He looked around for the individual and then noticed the person was now at the top of the second landing. He could now see that it was a man looking down at him but could not figure out how the guy had gotten from the bottom of the lower stairway all the way to the top of the second in the amount of time it had taken him to get over to the lower landing. Even if the man had run full speed, he shouldn't have been able to make it up that far. When the guard finally reached the second level, the man was nowhere to be found.

The guard looked up toward the very top of the Universal Stairway but didn't see the man, and by this time, he figured the person would be long gone, most likely hightailing it to the park exit to get away. As the employee turned to go back down the two flights of stairs, he looked down and saw that the man he had been following was now down at the very bottom, back in the lower lot, looking up at him.

The security guard had no idea how the man had gotten past him. Even if the guy had been crouching down, hiding as the guard had gone past, he should have made some sort of noise going down the escalator. Now the guard hurried down the two levels to the bottom, trying to keep an eye on the intruder as he descended. Just as he was beginning to start down the final flight, the man turned and walked toward the entrance to the Revenge of the Mummy ride. Once the security guard reached the bottom of the escalator, he sprinted over to where he had seen the man walk but could find no trace of the intruder. The guard looked all over the area near the Mummy ride, but the man had disappeared. Once the guard had given up, he headed back toward the security room. As he glanced in the direction of the Universal Stairway, he once again spotted the man back up near

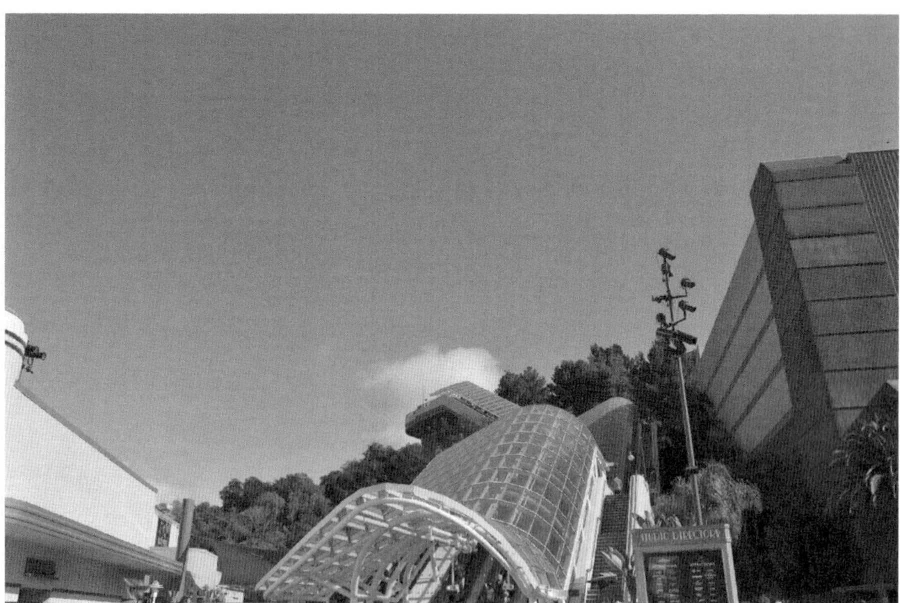

This is the view a security guard had when looking at a spirit who was playing tag with him.

the second landing. This time, however, the man was staring at him with a strange little smirk on his face. The guard was about to make his way back up the stairway when the man simply shook his head and faded into nothingness. The guard decided that he wasn't about to go chasing what he now realized was a ghost and continued on his way to the guard room.

This tale was confirmed by the other guard who was standing next to the man telling us the story. This other guard said that the same thing had happened to him in almost the exact same way. Both of these employees believe that the spirit they had seen was the same ghost who haunts the Halloween Horror Nights maze next to the Mummy ride. The fact that this spirit darts into the area where the maze is set up may confirm that; however, only these two employees would admit to seeing this ghost or have been the only ones to have actually seen the spirit. We just don't know. Hopefully, the identity of this spirit will one day be known.

9
Ghosts of the Upper Lot

The upper lot at Universal Studios was formed when Caltrans needed dirt for the construction of the Hollywood Freeway, and for the free dirt, Universal got a flat-topped hill to build the now famous upper lot, which is the hub of the theme park. This section of the park is where the Universal CityWalk is located, along with the ticket booths, entryway, shows, shops and the ever-popular Wizarding World of Harry Potter. In essence, the upper lot is the heart of the amusement park.

The upper lot, or the Entertainment Center, is where you will find the majority of the theme park rides, theaters, shows and food establishments. Rides include Despicable Me: Minion Mayhem, The Simpsons ride and the many children's rides and attractions in Super Silly Fun Land, along with the exceedingly popular Harry Potter and the Forbidden Journey experience, which takes riders through a quidditch-infused adventure in and around Hogwarts with Harry, Hermione and Ron as companions. The upper lot is also where you will find hit shows such as the special effects show, Water World and the new Walking Dead maze that takes guests through a zombie-infested world of horror. There are also plenty of food choices here with the Three Broomsticks—fast becoming the favorite—as well as Luigi's Pizza, Gru's Café and even Lard Lad Donuts for those who want to munch on the run. Hamburgers and hot dog stands are an easy find as well. There is an endless supply of things to do here in the Entertainment Center—perhaps this is why the area also has its fair share of spirits wandering its themed streets and enjoying its thrilling rides.

TAKING STOCK

For those who enjoy shopping for souvenirs, Universal Studios has a plethora of marketplaces within the theme park. The first of these shops you encounter upon entering the park itself is the huge Universal Studio Store. Here you will find merchandise ranging from *The Simpsons* and Harry Potter and all the way back to the golden age of monster movies and, for employees, spirits who have claimed the basement stockroom for their own.

On our first visit to Universal Studios, we tried to talk to as many employees as we could, and the Studio Store, being so close to the entrance, was our first stop. When we asked two clerks who were standing behind a cash register if they knew of any ghost stories regarding the park, they quickly glanced at each other in what was obviously a nervous way. When they turned back, one of them cleared his throat and asked if we wanted to hear about something that happens in the basement of the store. Since this is a book about all the ghost activity, we told them we definitely wanted to hear their tale.

The male clerk told us that he had gone down to the basement late one night after the park had closed with a list of things that needed to come up to replenish the shelves from the day's sales. When he got to the door, he found that it wouldn't open; no matter how hard he tried, he couldn't get the door to budge. He started back up to the showroom floor, but just as he started out, he heard the door behind him give a slight creak. When he glanced back, he saw that the door was slowly opening. He didn't really think much about it, figuring that the door had just been stuck and he had managed to break it free just as he was giving up on it.

The employee began gathering the items needed when he heard something move behind him. He noticed that a box had been dislodged from its spot and had moved into the center of the aisle he was in. He quickly placed the box back where it belonged and continued his work. He then moved to another section of the stockroom, and again, while he was gathering his items, he heard movement directly behind him and saw that another box was now in his way. He now thought to himself that the odds of this happening twice, in two different walkways, was rather remote, but he again moved the container back to its proper spot and headed for the exit to go back up the stairs.

As the employee neared the door, a box that was on one of the lower shelves slid out in front of him, blocking his way. The startled man looked around to see if someone was down there with him playing a prank, but

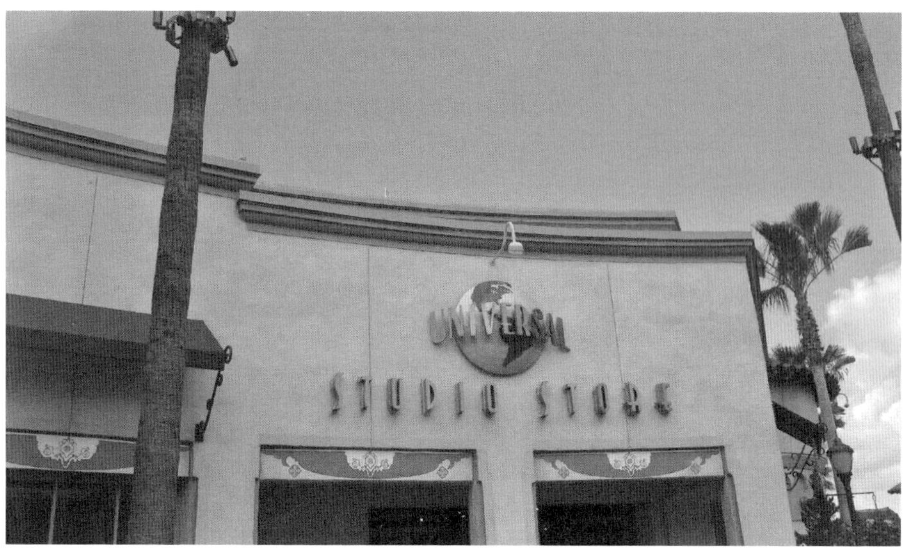

The Studio Store near the theme park entrance may well be the most haunted place in the park.

he couldn't find anybody. He moved the box back to its original place and had started walking again when another box, this one higher up than the first, slid out and down in front of him, again blocking his way. This time, however, the clerk slid the box just far enough aside that he could get past and sprinted for the door. As he was dashing up the stairs, he clearly heard the door behind him shut with a thud.

The man had heard stories from some of his co-workers that the basement was haunted but had figured the tales were either meant to scare him or were just things that the others had heard themselves and were merely passing along. Now, he had proof that the stories he was told were true and hoped he would never have to go back into the basement again. Unfortunately, restocking the shelves is a part of his job, but if he is required to go to the basement he now makes sure he is not alone.

Once the male clerk was finished telling us his story, the female clerk began hers. She said that what happened to her is a common occurrence down in the stockroom, with quite a few employees complaining about it, so much so that the store now recommends that no one go down there alone. Her story starts off the same way as her co-worker's in that she needed to go down into the stockroom to replenish items sold that day. She had no trouble getting into the room and didn't have any boxes launch themselves at her. However, while she was retrieving the items she needed, she heard the distinct sound of a heavy object moving near where the door to the basement was located. Like her co-worker, she really didn't give it much thought, thinking that another employee had come down and needed to move something to get what he or she had come for. This was not the case.

After the girl had picked up the items she needed, she went back to the door and found that it was blocked by a box that was so big and so heavy that she couldn't move it. No matter how hard she tried, the box wouldn't budge. The clerk tried to call upstairs to her co-workers, but being down in the basement, she didn't have any reception. Yelling didn't work, as no one could hear her, so the only thing she could do was wait and hope that someone would come down before everyone went home for the night. Luckily it didn't take long, but it did take considerable effort by three men to get the door open and let her out. To this day, the clerk refuses to go back into the basement alone.

Another story we heard on a recent trip to the park had to do with the old office and employee breakroom area. A former manager told us that he had been working late one evening when he heard one of his employees let out a scream. He rushed back to see if she was alright, but before he could get to the back room, he found the young woman and one of her co-workers rushing out of the area. He told us that both of the women look frightened and when he was finally able to get them to tell him what happened, he was surprised at what they said. He told us that the girl who screamed had been holding a hanger in her hand and was about to place it down on a table when the hanger violently flew from her hand and hit the wall opposite from where they were standing. They said that it hit the wall so hard that it put a dent in the plaster. Upon inspection, the manager found the hanger lying on the floor next to the wall and there was an imprint in the wall where it had hit. The manager said that neither of the women would go back into that area of the store ever again.

Another story the former manager told us had to do with an office in the back of the store. He said that many employees would see a man sitting at the table in the room busily typing away on an invisible typewriter. The man would never turn around and would never even acknowledge their presence but just continued to type. As soon as the employees would walk into the room, the man simply vanished. The former manager said that this phantom typist became so common that most of the employees would just ignore the ghost and go about whatever business they were doing. The manager did tell us that he had never seen the phantom himself but had heard the story from so many of the employees that he figured it must be true.

Look Out

Tragedy can strike anywhere and at any time, even in a happy place like Universal Studios. When a person is struck with severe depression or other mental illness, that tragedy can manifest as self-destructive behavior and the need to eliminate that which is perceived to be the cause of that depression. This is exactly what happened on April 3, 2015.

On that fateful day in April, a young man, distraught over losing his girlfriend, went to the theme park to confront his former partner about their breakup. The couple had a child together, and the split had hit the man hard. The woman, who was an employee at one of Universal Studios' restaurants, had already taken out several restraining orders on her estranged boyfriend, but that was not going to stop him from seeing her. On this day, however, he had decided that one way or another he was going to put an end to the situation and arrived at the theme park determined to see it done.

As the young man nervously paced the area next to his estranged partner's workplace, trying to figure out his next move, his ex noticed him from a window and called park security. Because the restaurant was located next to the children's area of the park, security was not taking any chances with the

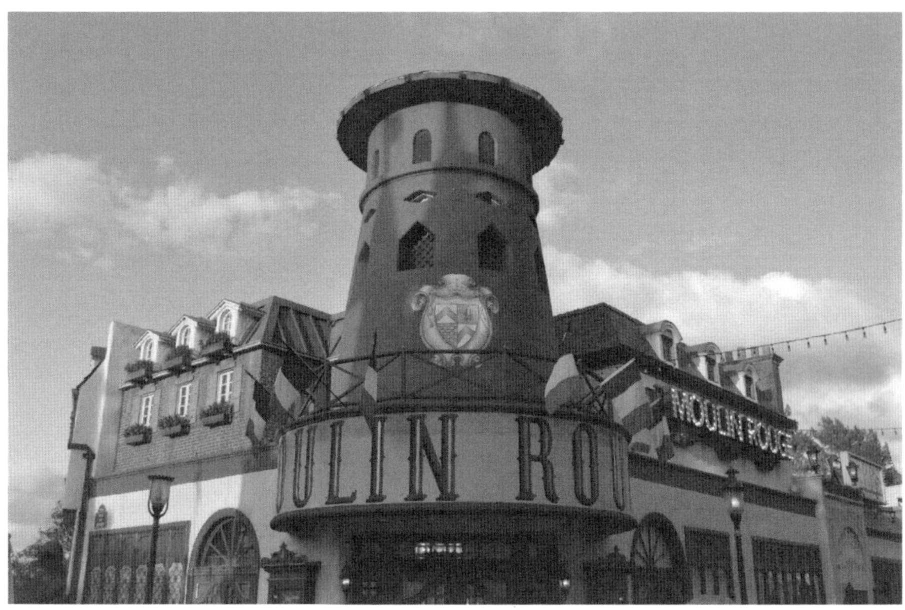

This VIP restaurant is where the girlfriend of a suicidal young man worked.

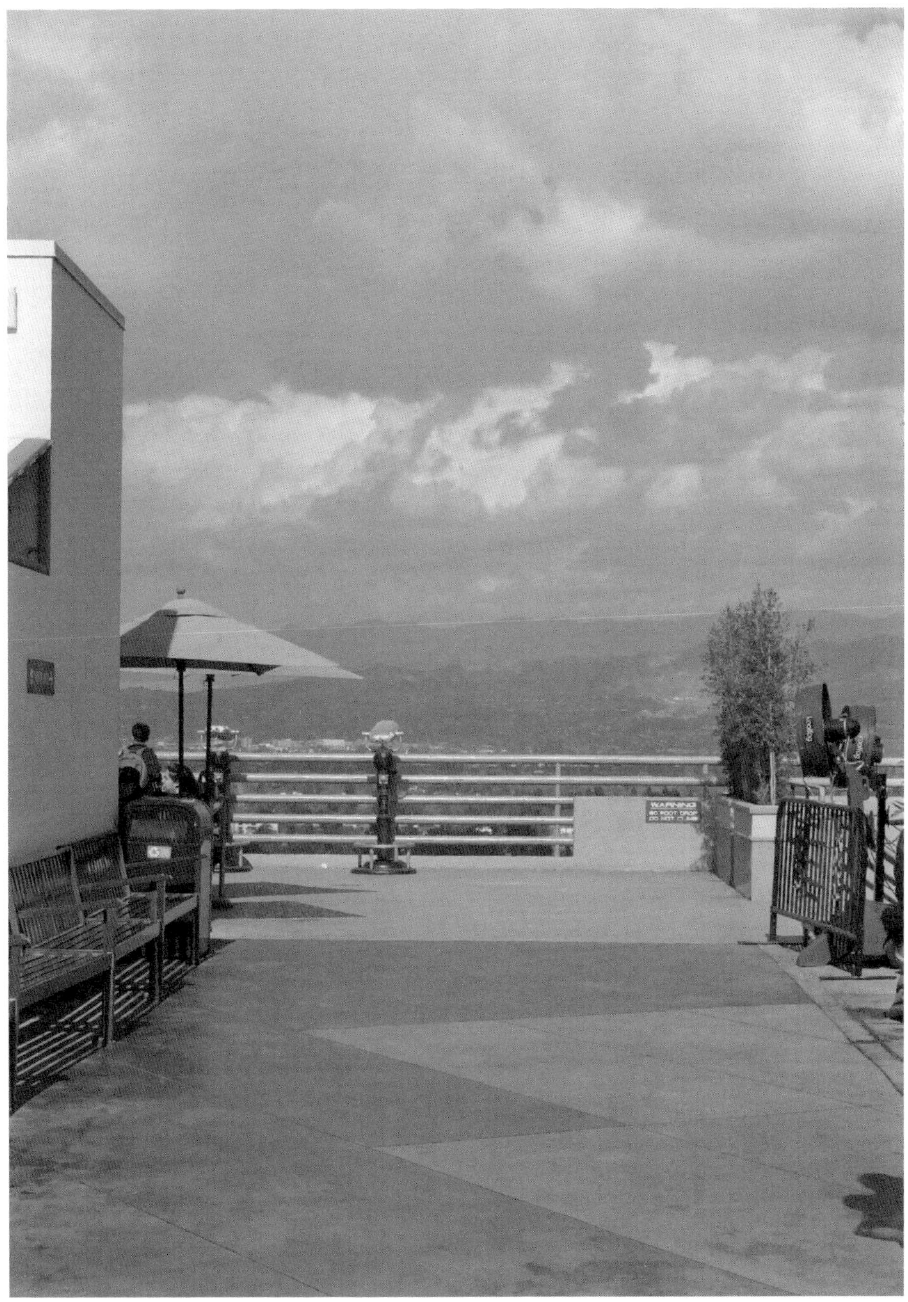

This is the overlook where police confronted an armed young man.

safety of its guests and called the Los Angeles County Sheriff's Department. When the officers arrived, they were immediately escorted to the young man's location, but the sight of the police made him quite agitated, and no matter how hard the officers tried, they couldn't calm him down. Unfortunately, the man was in no mental shape to cooperate, and as the officers came near, he quickly pulled out a pistol, placed it to his temple and pulled the trigger. He died instantly from the gunshot. This is not the end of the man's story, however. Since that day, strange things have been happening near the area where the young man committed suicide.

Some of the employees we talked to told us that a spirit is seen leaning up against the rail of the overlook. They can tell that it is a young man, but he seems to be completely oblivious to everything around him. He just stares out over the cliff face, looking down at the lower lot or off into the distance in the direction of the nearby mountains. These employees have stated that many of them have tried to approach the man, but every time someone gets too near, the spirit fades from view.

The overlook where the man committed suicide is directly adjacent to the area of the park designated for younger guests. The Super Silly Fun Land is close to the viewing area, separated only by a water play zone that allows children to get exceedingly wet. Because of this, Universal has installed a locker room where parents and guardians can keep towels, a change of clothes and any other item they might need to make sure their kids are comfortable after a prolonged soaking. This area, including the locker room and bathroom, have had reports of this young man wandering around as if in a daze. He never approaches anyone but will gaze at the kids in an almost fatherly way. People who know the story wonder if he is thinking about his child and how he will never be a part of the young one's life. Again, if he is approached in this area, he will simply vanish from view.

The entrance to the Super Silly Fun Land is another spot where this lost soul is seen. Here, the man is simply found walking into the children's amusement zone. The odd thing about this occurrence is the fact that he is seen moving only a short distance into the area before disappearing, reappears outside the kid's section and again walks in, once more vanishing from view. No one can remember him going into this section before he took his own life, so why he would continue to be seen doing this is a mystery.

There is one other place this man has reportedly been seen, but the employee who told us this could not verify that the story he heard was true or just a tale told by a co-worker to try and scare him. What we were told was that this young man is occasionally seen sitting at one of the tables at Gru's

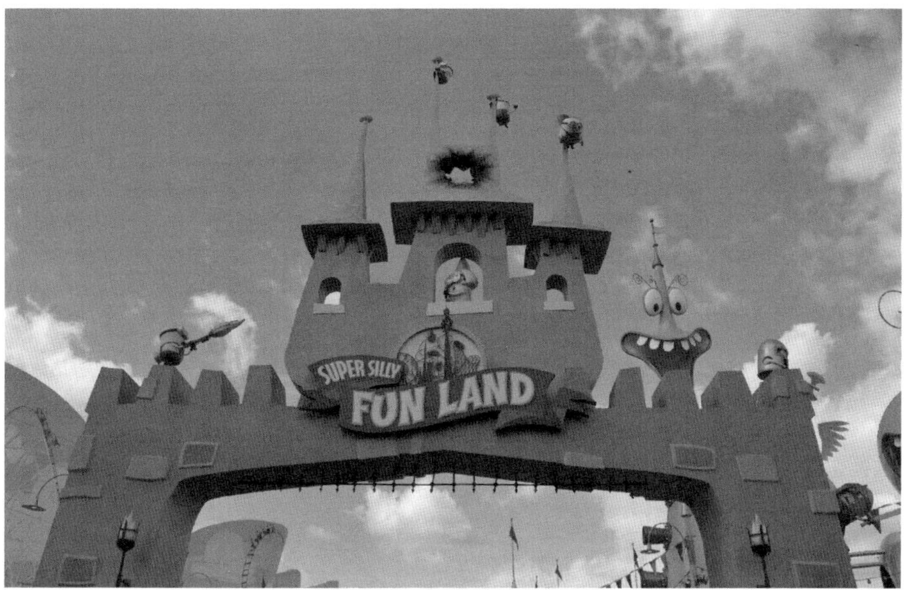

The spirit of a desperate young man is seen wandering near this area of the upper lot.

Café. The employee said that the entity is never seen at the same table or is there any particular time. The employee was told that when the man does show up in the eatery, he is seen in solid form and not as a ghost or spirit would appear. He was told that if anyone approaches the table where he is sitting, he will simply disappear and not return for days or weeks. This is one of those stories that the readers will have to decide for themselves whether or not it is true.

One thing seems clear about this spirit: he seems unsure of what is happening around him or to him. This is common in cases of suicide. The young man has never been frightening or aggressive toward any guest or employee, and it seems clear that he is just lost and possibly looking for answers.

Little Girl Lost

The Simpsons ride at Universal Studios is one of the most popular at the theme park. This motion-based CGI roller coaster simulator takes guests on a wild ride through Krustyland as an escaped Sideshow Bob tries to kill them using all kinds of devious twists and turns of the coaster car. As popular as this ride is, however, it didn't start off using *The Simpsons* as its theme. It began life as the Back to the Future ride, with Steven Spielberg as its greatest champion. When the closure of this ride was announced in the spring of 2007, there were many fans who were upset about the closure and even considered a petition drive to stop it, but in the end, the Back to the Future ride closed on September 3, 2007. There was one fan who decided that the ride, in whatever iteration it took, was going to remain her home regardless of whether she was dead or not.

The Back to the Future ride was similar to what the creators of the new attraction had in mind; it was a first-generation CGI motion simulator that took guests on a trip through time in an eight-passenger DeLorean while Doc Brown tried to keep them safe with the same absentminded style we know from the movies. Being a first-gen ride, the smoothness we know today was lacking, and the sharp twists and turns of the cars could take their toll on riders by causing motion sickness, dizziness and other ailments. Once the new ride came into being, all of that changed, and the ride became much more rider friendly. Regardless of how the ride could make one lose his or her lunch, it had a steadfast fan base, including a ghostly little girl.

Even when Back to the Future was still in operation, guests and employees would see the girl on occasion, usually riding in one of the DeLoreans but always alone. Many of those who witnessed her would question the ride employees about the little girl who seemed unattended by parent or adult. At first, the employees were at a loss—none of them could remember checking in an unaccompanied minor into the ride or remember seeing one exit once the ride was finished. It is Universal's policy not to allow small children to ride the attractions without a parent or a responsible party, and the park is strict in keeping to this safety procedure. There were many times after a patron reported seeing this little girl that an employee, knowing that she had not exited, would go back through the ride and search for the child, but she was never found. So many times was this girl reported that she became an urban myth among the employees at Universal Studios—that is, until she was finally spotted by a ride technician while closing the attraction up one night.

One evening after the ride had closed, an employee was doing the final walk-through to make sure no one had been left inside and that the ride had been cleaned properly. While he was just finishing up, the employee heard someone giggle. It sounded like the laughter of a small girl, and the employee was afraid that a child had been inadvertently left behind by a parent. He was confused, however, because the ride had been closed for more than half an hour and figured that by that time, either the parents would have realized they had left their child behind or the kid herself would have come looking for help. The employee looked around but didn't see anyone, so he figured that the kid may have been scared and was hiding somewhere out of sight. The employee called out to the child, telling her that it was OK, she was safe and to come out so they could find her mother and father. Nothing. The man looked for a while longer but without any luck decided to go get some help from his co-workers. The employee headed for the exit door, and just as he was about to put his hand on the latch, he heard the giggling once again.

The man thought he knew where the girl was hiding judging by where the laughter seemed to be coming from, but when he arrived at the ride car in question, he found it empty. His confusion must have been amusing because she began to giggle again; this time, it sounded like it was coming from the ride car directly next to the one he had been looking in. He quickly went to the other car but again found it empty. Now, he heard the laughter coming from the car on the opposite end of the ride. He had no idea how the child could have gotten that far away from him so quickly but, not wanting her to get away again, sprinted to the cars on the other side before she could flee.

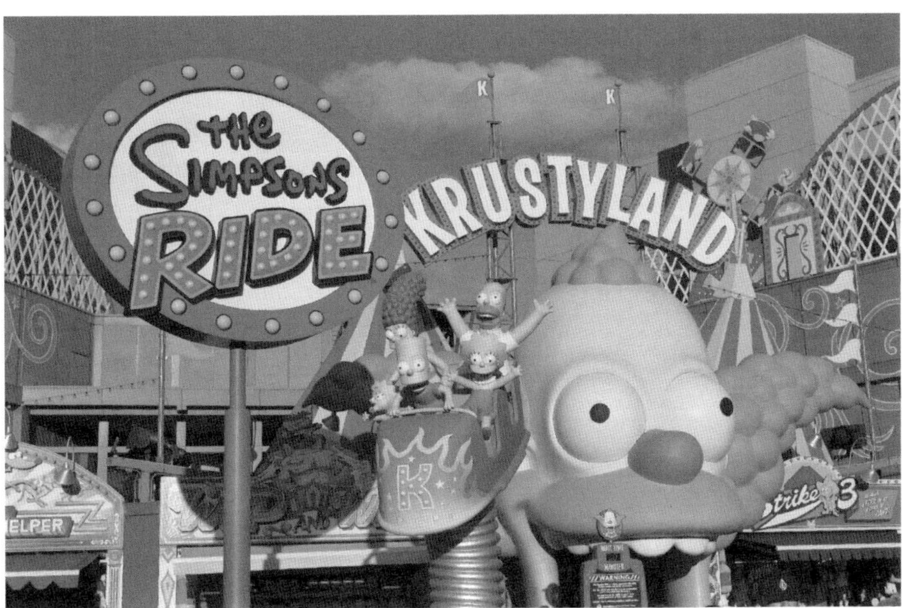

The Simpsons ride is haunted by a playful little girl who has also become a park legend over time.

However, he once again found the ride area empty with no sign of the little girl. Once more, the man heard the giggling but now it was back in the area he had just come from. He knew that there was no way the child could have gotten past him this time.

As the man dashed back to the other side of the ride zone his mind went to the stories he had heard of the little ghost girl who supposedly haunted the ride. He had always figured that it was just the myth that his co-workers always said it was since no one working at Universal had ever actually seen the child; now, he was beginning to think that maybe she actually did exist.

When the employee got to the place where he had heard the giggling, he couldn't find a soul. It was almost as if the child were playing hide and seek with him. As soon as he thought about hide and seek, the giggling started again, but this time, it was close to him and seemed to be coming from the area in front of the ride screen. The man turned to look where the laughing was coming from, and he saw a young girl standing in front of him. He let out a sigh of relief, thinking that he had found the lost little girl and smiled at her to reassure her that he was there to help. The girl was smiling back at him, and he could tell that she was, at the least, comfortable with him. The employee started walking toward the girl and told her that they would find her parents and have her back home in no time when the child gave him a big playful grin and dashed off—right through the wall.

The employee was stunned; he couldn't quite grasp what he had seen and just stood staring at the spot where the girl had vanished. It took him awhile to realize what had happened and who or what he had seen but finally came to grips with the idea he had just seen the ghost that he thought was nothing more than a story told to scare new hires. Now, however, he knew the tales were true, and he may have been the first employee to ever actually see the spirit. But he wouldn't be the last.

The Back to the Future ride was closed soon after the employee had first seen the spirit of the little girl. No one knew what would happen to her after the new ride was built, and many figured that she would probably just fade away into memory. That was far from what happened. Many of us in the paranormal field know that renovations do not mean that paranormal activity subsides and may actually make the activity increase. The sightings of this little girl did not get any more frequent, but they didn't go away either.

Over the years that The Simpsons ride has been open, many of the same reports that occurred before have remained: guests exiting the ride with concerns about the small child they had seen who was without an adult and riders wondering why they couldn't find the girl after the ride was over even

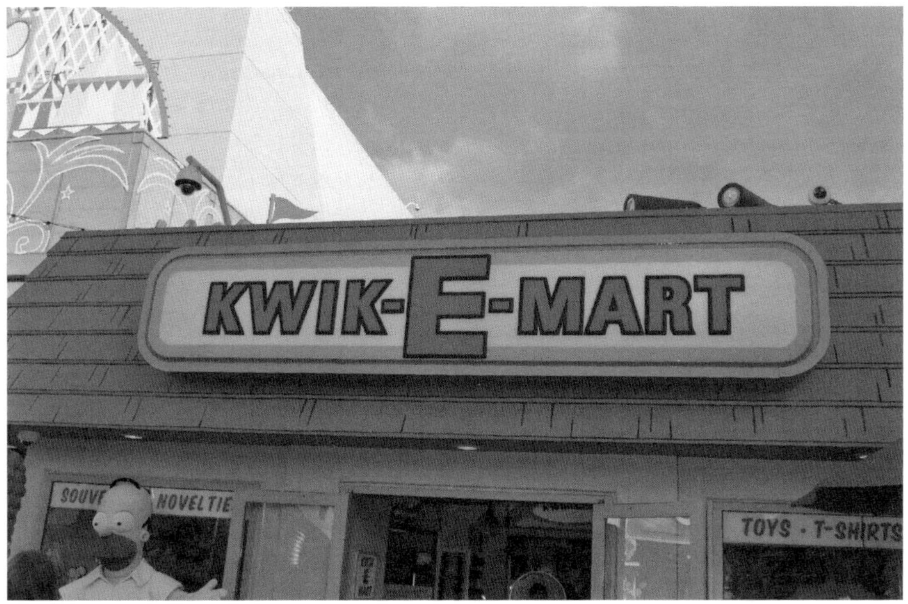

The same little girl who haunts The Simpsons ride is believed to haunt this store out front of the ride as well.

though they had been keeping an eye out for her to make sure she got off the ride safely. The only thing that has really changed now that the new ride has opened is that the employees working The Simpsons ride know that the little ghost girl is real—she seems to have gotten more comfortable showing herself to them. Many times, as they are closing the ride up for the night, the child will make herself known and wants to play with them. We found that those working the ride are not shy about talking about this little spirit, so we figure that they are talking about her to the guests. Who this lost little girl is no one is sure, but she seems to be a sweet child who is just looking for a playmate or friend. Hopefully someday we will find out exactly who she is and help her pass on—or at the very least call her by name to let her know she is not forgotten.

The store out in front of The Simpsons ride may be another place where our lost little girl likes to play. Once known as the Time Travelers Depot when the Back to the Future ride was still in operation, Kwik-E-Mart is now a themed candy and gift shop catering to all things Simpsons. We talked with one employee who told us that upon opening up for the day, he entered the small store and found that all of the items had been moved from their original places. Not just one or two items—every single thing in the shop had been moved. It took him and his co-workers an extra hour to open up, and he said that while they had been putting everything back in order, they kept hearing a little girl's laughter. They couldn't find where it was coming from but could tell that it emanated from inside the store. The employee went on to say that things have a tendency to fall off the shelves for no reason or get moved in the middle of the day, and the date on the computer receipts will mysteriously change. It would seem that our lost little girl has a mischievous streak to her, but as nothing is ever more than a prank, it is all in good fun.

A GHOSTLY PRODUCTION

There was one more tale told to us by two employees; however, they couldn't seem to agree on where exactly the phenomenon took place. One clerk said that it occurred in Feature Presentation directly across from the Studio Store, while the other employee swore that it happened in Production Central. The story is an interesting one, and because we aren't sure where it took place, we are going to assume it happened in the store where the two employees were working when they related it to us. That would be Production Central.

According to the two people, they were working in the store just after noon, and the crowd in the store was beginning to pick up. They were taking turns helping guests who had questions and manning the cash register for those with purchases when one of them noticed that the mannequin in the store had been moved. It was supposed to be facing the front of the shop but was now turned away from the entrance and facing the back wall. The clerk said that when he got a moment, he went and moved the mannequin back into position and then resumed helping the guests. The other employee had noticed her co-worker moving the figurine and had just assumed that an unruly guest had moved it thinking it would be funny.

Only about ten minutes after the clerk rearranged the mannequin, he glanced back over at it and found that it had once again been moved to face the back of the store. This time, the employee looked around the shop to see if he noticed anyone who looked familiar. He thought someone might be playing tricks on him and hiding in the store somewhere and then moving the figure when he and his co-worker weren't looking. He didn't see anyone who looked familiar or anyone who looked guilty hiding outside, so he went

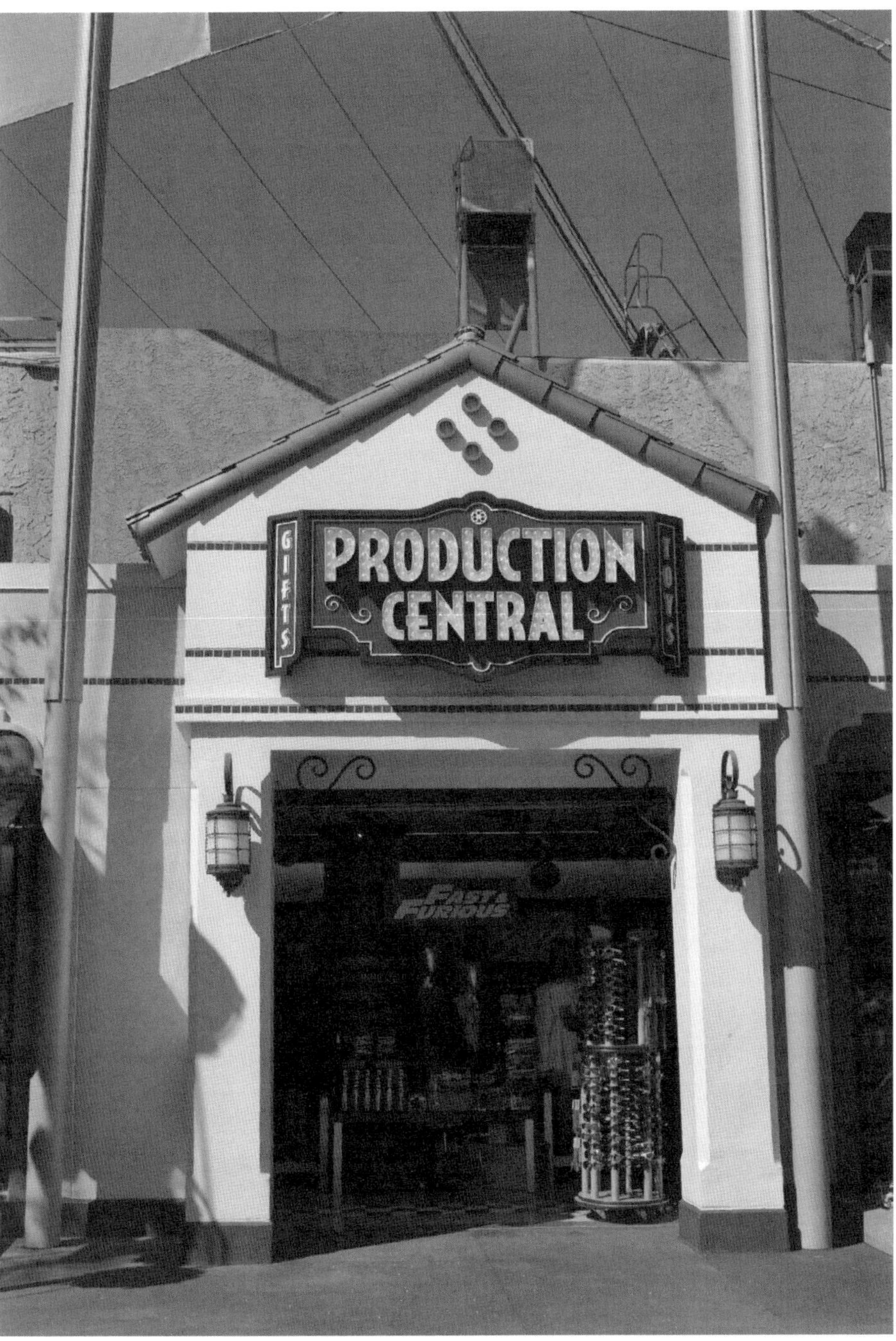

Production Central. It was in this gift shop that a mannequin moved of its own volition.

back in, moved the mannequin once again and then told his co-worker to keep an eye on the dummy. If someone was trying to play a prank on them, then they would catch the culprit.

Once the early afternoon crowd had thinned out and the two clerks could take a breather, they were talking behind the cash register when one of them saw that the mannequin was once again facing backward. Both of them swore to each other that they had been keeping a close eye on the figurine for the last hour or so and hadn't seen anyone messing with it. How then had it been completely turned in the opposite direction from the way it should be facing? The clerk who had been placing the dummy back to its proper position once more went over and moved it; this time, when he turned to walk back to the register, he heard his co-worker let out a gasp. When he asked her what happened, she just pointed to the mannequin that he had just moved. When the young man looked at the figurine, it was facing the back wall of the store once more. The employee hadn't heard a thing, but his co-worker told him that she had just seen it turn all on its own. The employee thought his co-worker was having fun with him and scoffed at her, when, out of the corner of his eye, he saw that the mannequin was moving. Both he and the other clerk turned to watch the figurine rotating back to where it was supposed to be facing. They looked at each other, and both bolted for the exit of the store.

Once outside in the bright sunlight of the day, they realized that they had left the shop completely unattended. Neither wanted to go back into the store but had no choice in the matter. They couldn't very well leave the shop with no one to look out for it and no one to attend to the guests who were going to come and look for souvenirs. Reluctantly, both of the dedicated employees reentered the shop and resumed their duties. We were told that once the clerks went back in, both of them looked at the mannequin and asked that it not move for the rest of their shift and asked that it please not scare them or their customers. They were both relieved when the figure stayed put, and since that day, neither of them has seen the mannequin move again.

The two employees also told us about a story they had heard that came from a friend of theirs who worked in Feature Presentation, near the park entrance. This store stocks a large amount of Harry Potter merchandise, including Chocolate Frogs. It seems that there is a spirit in this shop that likes to knock the frogs off of the shelves and then make the boxes jump around on the floor. After we heard this tale, we walked down to Feature Presentation to speak with the employees there, but none of them would

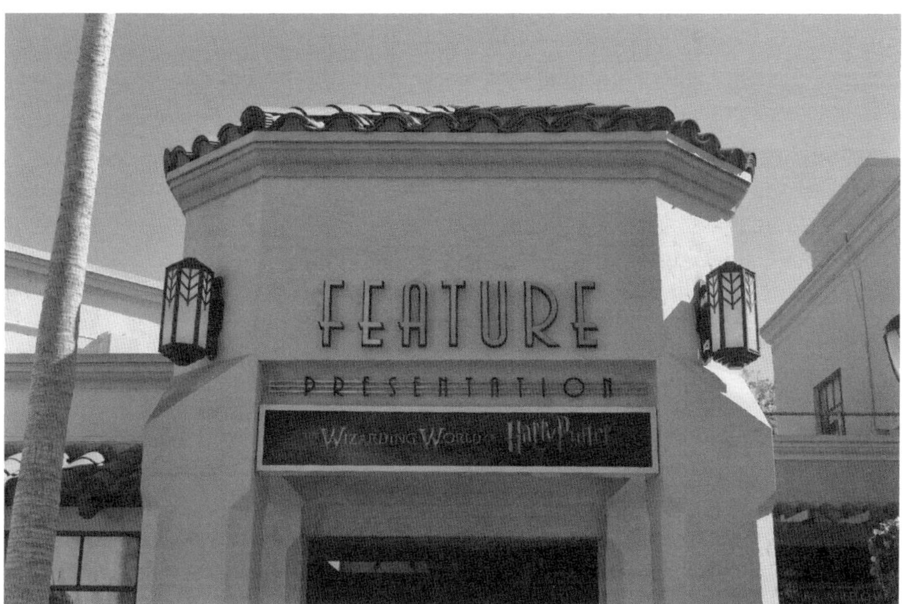

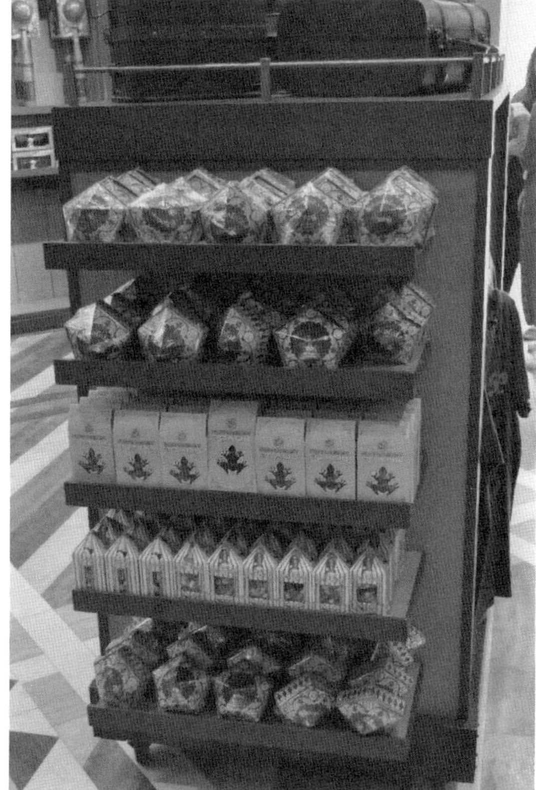

Above: Feature Presentation. In this store, the Chocolate Frogs refuse to stay on the shelves.

Right: This display is where the Chocolate Frogs randomly fall off the shelves and dance on the floor.

admit to the story. However, it should be noted that one of the managers said that the reason the Chocolate Frogs kept falling off of the shelves was because they were chocolate and therefore the candy would expand and shrink depending on the temperature, which caused them to fall to the floor. It would appear that this chocolate phenomenon only happens in this one store, so one has to wonder. To us, it was almost the same as admitting to the story we heard, but we leave it to the readers to decide.

10

Ghosts of Universal CityWalk

Universal Studios didn't start out to compete with the theme parks of its more entertainment-minded neighbors, Disneyland and Knott's Berry Farm. But that is exactly what happened once Universal opened up its new Glamour Tram tours and began to realize that to make money, it would need to adapt into a daylong venue rather than the two-hour tour it was known for.

Over the years, the studio added more and more attractions and rides, shows such as the Wild West show rivaling that of Knott's Berry Farm and Water World, which was a spectacular special-effects show second to none. As the theme park grew, so did the crowds, but they were still relatively light compared to the other parks. One of the reasons for that had to do with the fact that Disney and Knott's also had a plethora of shops both in and outside of their parks where guests would visit and spend their hard-earned money. Universal couldn't compete with this shopping desire and needed to come up with a way to draw guests in who may not have wanted to enter the theme park proper.

The idea that Universal came up with was the Universal CityWalk section just outside the gates of the theme park entrance. This first-of-its-kind shopping district was opened in May 1993, then expanded in 2000 and serves as the entrance plaza from the parking lots and to funnel guests down three blocks of shopping, dining and entertainment venues both to and from the theme park. CityWalk itself has become a destination all its own and includes a nineteen-screen movie theater replete with an Imax screen, nightclubs, a leaping fountain for kids and more than thirty stores and thirty places to eat. It even offers indoor skydiving for the more adventurous types. Even though CityWalk is still relatively new to the Universal family of entertainment, it comes with one other feature that most people would be surprised to find here: spirits, who, for one reason or another, have decided to stay after their lives have ended.

Raiders of the Lost Commode

On one trip to Universal CityWalk, we decided to step into the Raiders Store to see if any of the employees had any knowledge of paranormal activity within the shopping district. This store is near the parking lot, so it was our first stop on this research trip. We spoke to a girl behind the counter who immediately smiled and told us that she knew of one spirit that inhabits the women's public restroom directly next to their shop.

The employee told us that she had been working the night shift a month or so back and needed to use the restroom; unfortunately, the employee bathroom was in use, so she told her co-worker to mind the store and headed to the public one next to the parking lot. She said that she was in the stall and heard someone come into the bathroom, open the stall next to hers and shut the door—then all was quiet. Too quiet. The girl said that it was an almost eerie silence that had enveloped the restroom, and she didn't hear a sound coming from the stall next to her even though she knew someone was using it. After all, she clearly heard someone enter but not leave the toilet.

The girl decided to take a peek under the side wall of her stall but didn't see anyone's legs or feet when she looked. She knew that the person hadn't left the stall, which meant that the person was either very, very short-legged or was up on the seat hiding her legs. Regardless of the reason, the employee was nervous about the situation, finished up quickly and left her stall. As she was hurriedly washing her hands, she kept an eye on the occupied stall door in the mirror to see if it would open, who might come out and if she needed to make a run for the exit. As she was drying her hands, she saw that the stall door was beginning to slowly open but she couldn't see anyone coming out. Just as she was about to turn away, the employee said that the stall door burst open, slamming hard against the metal wall of the stall next to it, making a loud clanging sound. No one came out of the stall, however, and the girl could see that the stall was empty.

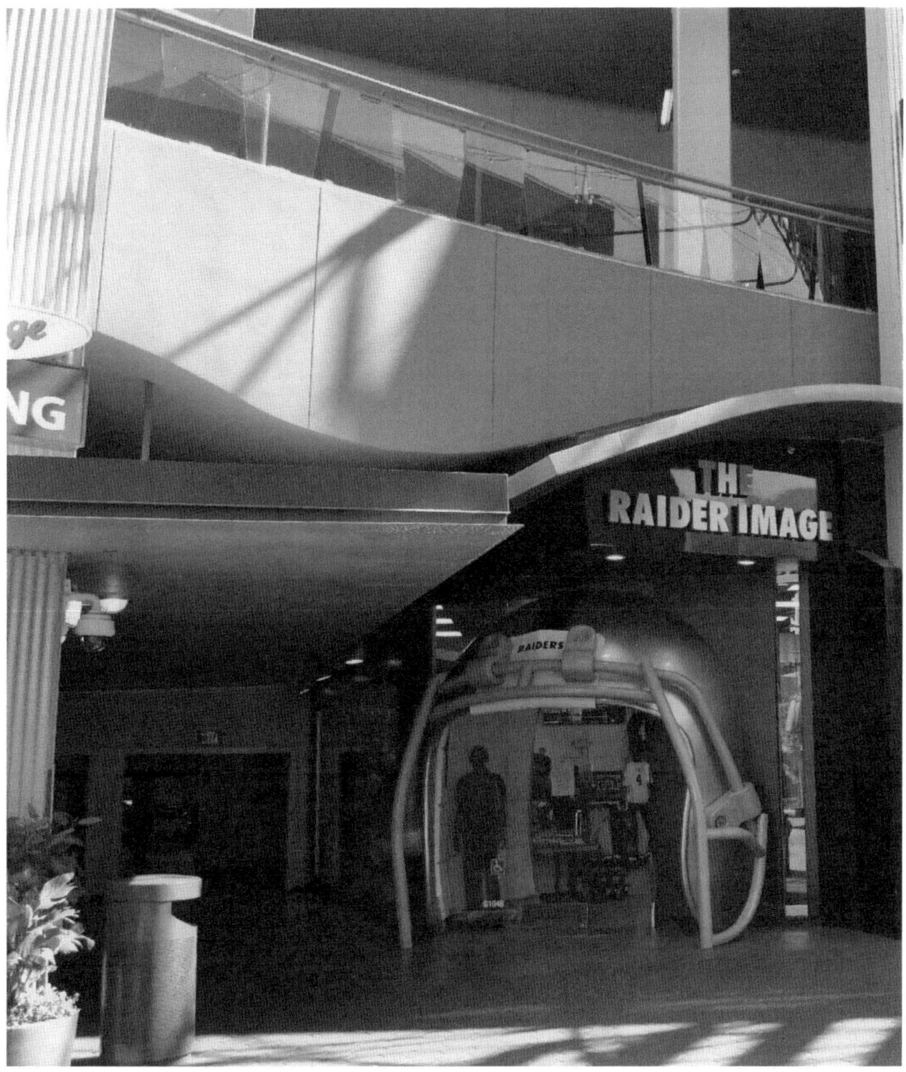

The Raiders Store at Universal CityWalk.

The Raiders Store employee said that even though she was now scared half to death, she was curious about how the stall door could have been pushed open so hard and how the person she knew should have been in the toilet could have gotten out without her knowing about it. As she cautiously approached the stall, she realized that there was no way the person could have gotten out, no other door in the cubicle, no way to go over the top or

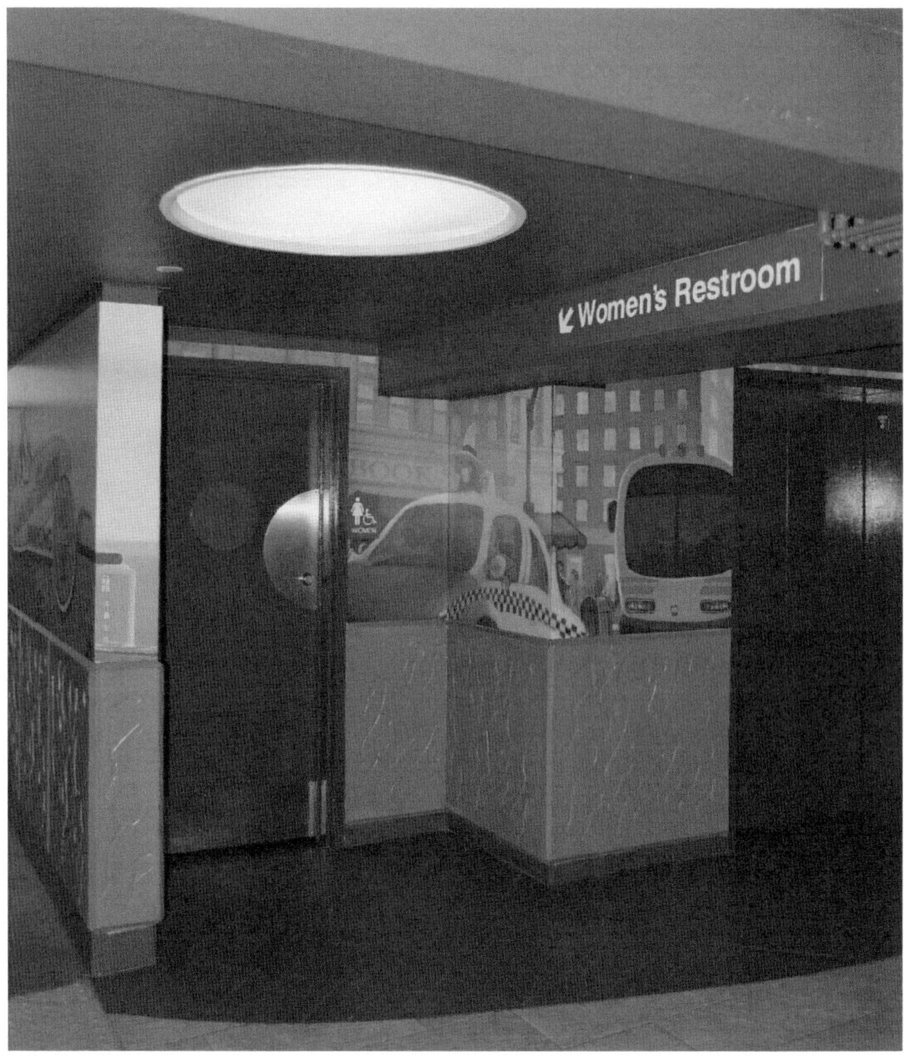

This women's restroom near the parking lot of Universal CityWalk is said to be haunted by an unknown spirit.

under the stall without her knowing. Just as she was about to stick her head into the stall to take a closer look, the door began to rock, and as she pulled her head back, the door slammed shut. The stunned girl stepped back, and as she did so, the door began to violently open and close. The employee had had enough and bolted for the outside door; according to her, the stall door was still slamming open and closed as she made it to the hallway and back to the safety of the Raiders Store. The girl said that after that night, she would never use that restroom again.

We have been back to CityWalk many times since this girl told us her story but could not find anyone else who works at the Raiders Store or any of the other nearby businesses to corroborate her tale, so we leave it up to the reader to decide. We did, however, have a guest come up to us who had overheard us questioning an employee who told us that there was indeed a spirit in the women's bathroom. This woman said that even though she has never come across the spirit herself, she, as a psychic, could feel her presence every time she passed that restroom.

As a side note, those of us who do paranormal investigations know that spirits seem to love bathrooms, attics and closets. We can only guess at why this is so, but the prevailing theory is that it has to do with the infrequency of the living interrupting them in whatever it is they are doing in the afterlife. Suffice it to say, almost every haunted location has a toilet ghost.

A Shot in the Dark

Whenever you have a popular entertainment district, particularly one that spans all aspects such as movies and music, things can happen that are out of the establishment's control. Young people can get out of hand in the heat of the moment, and when competition takes place, especially one involving DJs and music, tensions can run high in the heat of the moment. This is what happened one fateful night in May 2014 during one such competition at Infusion Lounge at Universal CityWalk.

On that cool spring night in May, LAPD responded to a group disturbance call, and when they arrived, found a large group of people pushing, shoving and creating a nuisance outside the Infusion Lounge nightclub. As the officers approached the crowd of young people, shots erupted from the group, and everyone took cover. The officers located the suspect, ordered him to drop the gun and fired when the young man didn't respond, killing him. The whole tragic incident could have been avoided if the man hadn't had the gun or had obeyed the police and put the gun down. Unfortunately, that is not what happened. Since that tragic night, tales of the spirit of a man have been reported dashing through the main walkway of CityWalk near where this incident had occurred. Even though Infusion Lounge has since closed, the spirit, who may be that of the young man killed by police, seems to still be here and trying to get away from something.

We first found out about this spectral runner on our first visit to CityWalk. From the closest store to the parking lots to the one nearest the theme park entrance, employee after employee told us about the ghost who runs through the entertainment district. Many have claimed to have seen him, and almost all of the stories are the same. The employee had a closing shift late at night, and after locking up and heading home, he or she would see the man dashing away down the walkway, always looking over his shoulder and always with a look of fear on his face. Witnesses only see him for a short period before he vanishes from sight, leaving them to wonder if they had actually seen a ghost or if their imaginations were playing tricks on them. One person we talked to did have a different tale to tell, one we couldn't verify, but it was a strange story, so we decided to tell it.

One night while closing up the shop (we were asked that the store not be named), this employee had to go back inside because he had left his keys on a backroom table. As he turned away from the front door of the shop, he saw what he thought was a man running down the walkway right out front but figured it was just another employee trying to hurry home. He had heard about the phantom runner but never really put much stock in stories of ghosts.

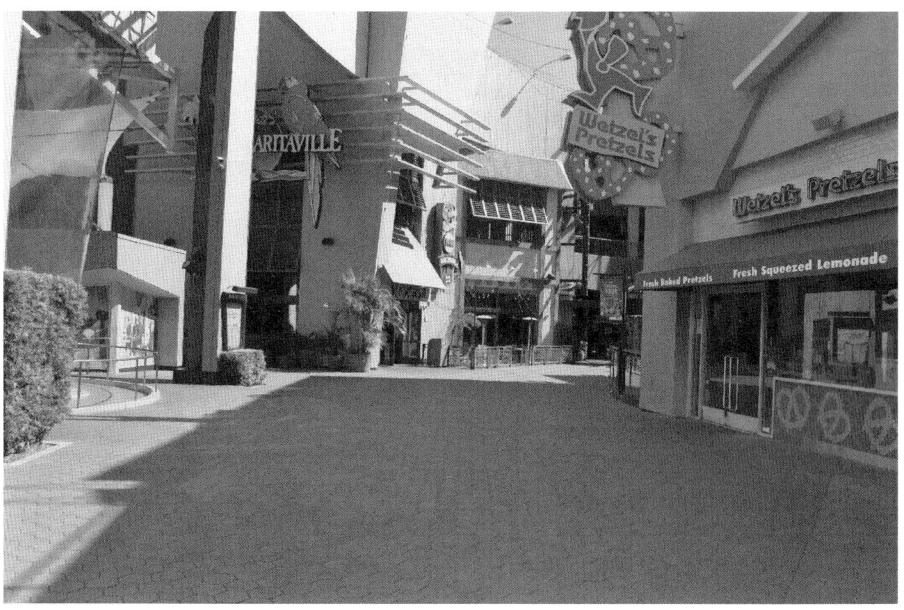

The spirit of a young man is seen running down this walkway at Universal CityWalk.

After he had retrieved the keys, he went back out front but was startled to see a man standing directly in front of the door. The person had his back to the store, but what rattled the clerk was that the man seemed to be transparent. As the employee stood there staring at the man, he kept wondering to himself if he had been wrong all this time in not believing in ghosts. He was still staring, unable to move, when the man at the door turned, looked at him and mouthed the words "help me." The clerk told us that he now knew that it was a ghost he was looking at and that he would never forget the look on the spirit's face—fear mixed with utter sadness. The employee remembers the feeling that came over him as he looked into the eyes of the spirit. He said that a wave of hopelessness came over him, a sense of despair that was almost more than he could cope with. He said it felt as if he were lost with no hope of ever being found, never able to see those he loved ever again.

He was still staring at the figure standing at the door when the spirit turned away and dashed down the walkway toward the parking lots at the other end. Once the spirit had departed, the feeling of loss and sadness went away as well. The employee told us that he has kept an eye out for the phantom ever since but hasn't seen him again. He said that if he ever had the chance, he would like to figure out a way to help the man but has no idea where to even start. He even asked us if there was anything we could do.

No one is quite sure who this poor soul is, but the assumption is that it's the young man who died that night in May. If it is this person, one can only hope that he will find peace. If someone does again make contact with him as the store clerk who told us this story did, please try to let the young man know that everything is alright, that he can move on without fear and without regret. For whatever you may believe, the afterlife will render peace and eternal rest.

MARIACHI MAYHEM

Camacho's Cantina is one of those restaurants that you go to not knowing what to expect but return time and time again because of the wonderful food, excellent service and great prices, not to mention the atmosphere and the fun of marvelous mariachi music. The one thing that guests at this now iconic Hollywood landmark might not expect are the ghosts.

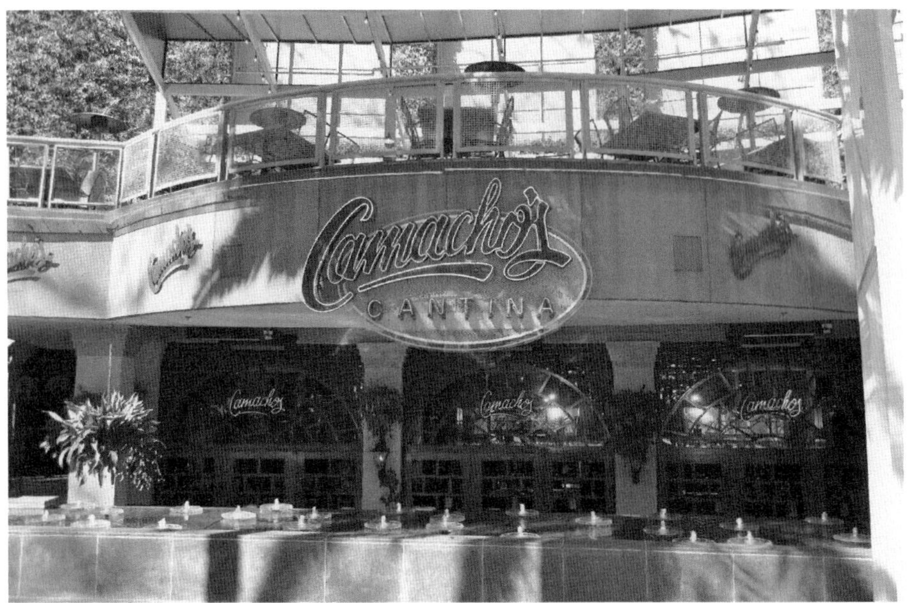

Camacho's Cantina has become a destination restaurant for Angelinos coming to CityWalk.

Camacho's had its start in 1984 when local attorney and businessman Andy Camacho purchased the El Paseo Inn Mexican restaurant on Olvera Street in downtown Los Angeles. Camacho was so successful running El Paseo that when Universal decided to create the CityWalk, the developers sought out Camacho to establish a traditional Mexican restaurant as an anchor in the courtyard, and Lew Wasserman himself suggested the name Camacho's Cantina for the new establishment. Soon after opening, Camacho's Cantina became a staple on the Hollywood scene and one of the most well-known Mexican restaurants in California. It's so well known, in fact, that at least one spirit has decided to take up residence in the cantina.

While dining at Camacho's, we mentioned to the waiter that we were writing this book, and almost conspiratorially, he leaned in and told us that the restaurant was haunted. It was just after the lunch rush at the cantina, and the crowd was extremely light, so after he took our order he came back and asked if we would like to hear a story—of course, the answer was yes.

The waiter said that one evening, a customer had gone into the bathroom but was in there for only a minute when he came running out looking frightened. One of the staff stopped him to ask if everything was alright, but the customer shook his head, said that the bathroom was moving and

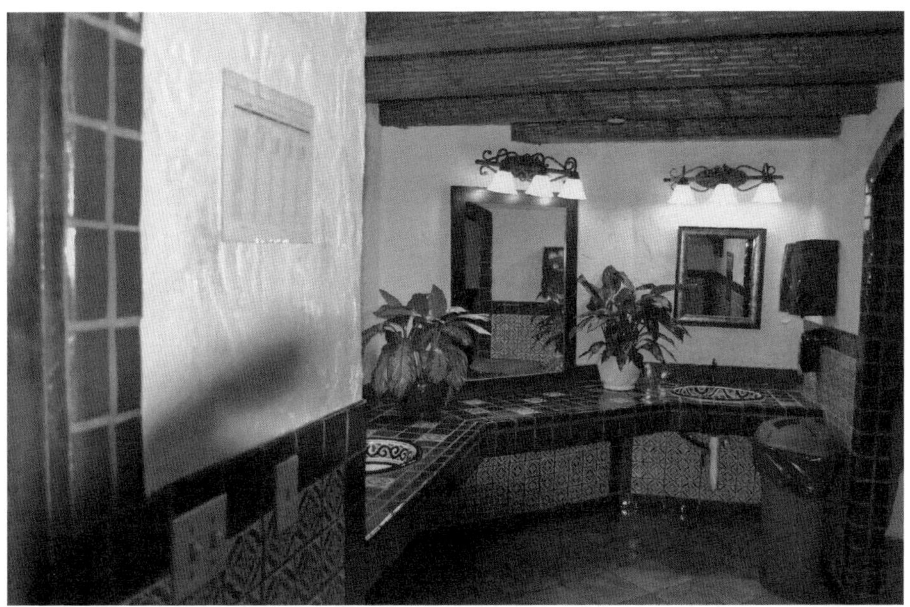

The haunted men's restroom at Camacho's Cantina.

then gathered up his family and left. The staff member who had stopped the man watched as the guest left and then headed to the bathroom himself to see what might have scared the man. When he came back, he said that he didn't find anything out of the ordinary and the staff wondered if the man had too many margaritas. The waiter told us that two more times that evening guests came out of the bathroom to tell one of the staff that there was something not right in there. Each time an employee would go into the restroom, nothing was found.

Later that night, after the restaurant had closed, the staff began to hear bangs and other noises coming from the men's bathroom. It was ignored for a time but became so constant that someone finally went to check to see what was happening. The employee came walking back almost immediately and told them all that they had to come look at what was going on. Our waiter told us that when he looked in the restroom, all of the faucets were turned on, the toilets were repeatedly flushing and one of the stall doors was slowly opening and closing—what they had been hearing from outside while cleaning up was the stall door, every once in a while, slamming shut before slowly opening and closing. No one knew quite what to do about the situation, so they all just went back to finishing their work so they could get

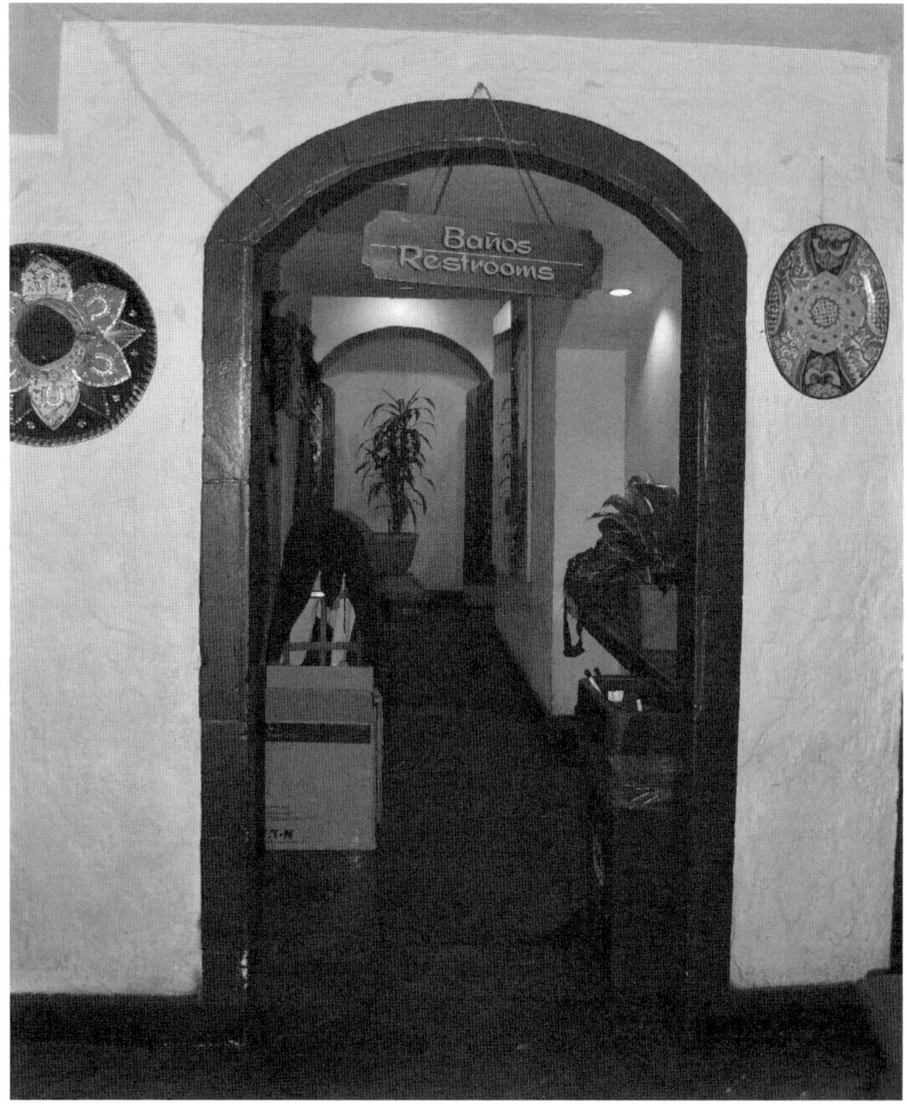

The entrance to Camacho's restrooms with the busser's station just to the left past the archway.

the hell out of there. He told us that this was the first time that anyone had an idea that the place might have been haunted.

The waiter also told us that the busser's station had an odd habit of making anyone standing near it dizzy. He said that it didn't happen often but that it could actually make people sick. Nothing serious, but enough to make the employee need to sit down for extended periods of time to get back to normal. He said that one waiter who had been standing at the station had actually become so dizzy that he passed out. He told us that it is common enough that when the phenomenon occurs, everyone will avoid the busser's station or make sure not to linger very long so they won't get sick themselves.

As we were leaving the cantina, we were approached by one of the managers, who had heard what we had been talking about and took us over to a mural on the wall behind the receptionist station. He told us about the history of the cantina and the Camacho family and then told us that the cantina was indeed haunted. He told us that many times when opening up the restaurant in the mornings the staff will find the tables all moved around, the chairs shoved into one corner or "stacked like something out of the movie *Poltergeist*." He also said there are times at night when he is the last to leave and locking up and has heard the tables and chairs moving.

No one knows who the spirit is or when exactly it arrived at the cantina, only that the restaurant is now haunted. The manager told us that even though the busser's station was a problem, the spirit has never tried to harm anyone and the moving around of furniture was more of a nuisance than anything else. He said that the spirit is just another aspect of the restaurant, and everyone is used to having it around, with some even having fun with the haunts by telling guests about the happenings.

The one thing we can tell you is, if you want a great Mexican meal while listening to good mariachi music, Camacho's Cantina will definitely fit the bill.

ROCKIN' THE HOUSE

The Hard Rock is one of those places where everyone loves to eat, to listen to good music and to shop for all sorts of Hard Rock paraphernalia. The Universal CityWalk Hard Rock is no different, except maybe for the ghost who likes to cause some harmless mayhem in the store adjacent.

On one of our first trips to CityWalk, we went into the Hard Rock store to ask if the employees had ever seen the spectral jogger making his way down the venue; it was one of the only stories we had heard from the entertainment area and figured it would be a good place to start. The clerk told us that he had no idea what we were talking about but mentioned that his co-worker

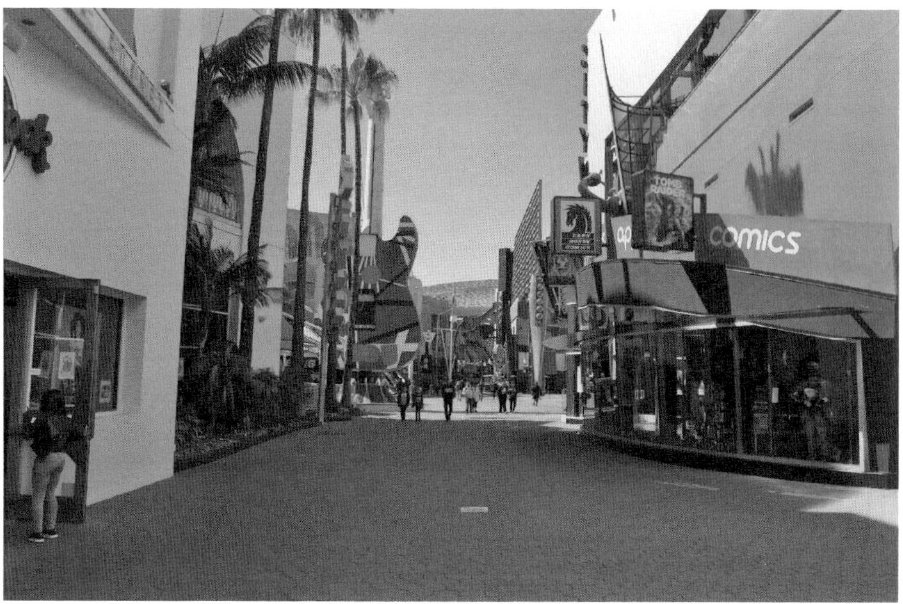

CityWalk with the Hard Rock store just visible on the left.

told him that the Hard Rock store was haunted. He had only been working at the shop for a couple of weeks so couldn't tell us anything, but if we would wait, he would get his co-worker.

When the other employee finally came out, he looked a bit apprehensive and said it was because he didn't know how Hard Rock would feel about us writing about the store being haunted, but we assured him that we would keep his name out of it. This seemed to alleviate his fears. He went on tell us about how things in the store would simply drop to the floor even when securely fastened to whatever shelf they were on. He said it didn't happen often but enough that anyone working at the store for any length of time knew that something odd was going on in the shop.

The employee told us that when he and one of his co-workers were working one afternoon, they both saw one of the displays on a table near the door move. His co-worker, who was an avowed nonbeliever in anything paranormal, went over to the display to move it back into position while mumbling something about the wind. As he turned back, an item on the shelf next to him fell off and hit the floor. Even though it was too heavy to have been moved by the wind, the employee couldn't be convinced otherwise. Just as this employee got back around the counter, the display that he had just repositioned moved again, but this time it turned a complete 180 degrees. The clerk told us that he tried to convince his co-worker that things like that do not happen due to the wind, but the guy just laughed and made fun of his believing in ghosts.

As the other employee started to walk back to straighten out the display once more, he was still laughing and making jokes about ghosts when it seemed like the entire store erupted. Just about everything in the shop was tossed off the shelves, the display the co-worker was heading for began to spin and the outside door actually closed on its own. The employee telling us this story said that even though he was shocked and disturbed by what had just happened, he started to laugh. He said that his co-worker had a look on his face of pure fright and had stopped dead in his tracks. It would seem that the spirit, whatever it was, didn't like being ignored or thought of as nonexistent. The employee told us that since that day, he would joke to the other employee about the spirit in the store but knew that his co-worker was now a complete believer.

11
Bonnie Vent's Story

In 2004, I was asked to film a promotional spot along with Butch Patrick, who played Eddie Munster, for CBS's upcoming *The Munsters* fortieth-anniversary DVD. I had arranged for Barris Kustom to bring a replica Munster car—or Koach, as it was called—to be used in the spot but was disappointed when we found out that we couldn't film in front of the old Munster house because of filming already scheduled.

On the day of the shoot, we were escorted to what is called Mediterranean Square. I had been getting a surreal feeling from the moment I set foot on the lot, but now, in this location, it amped up to another level. Once the interview started, we all had to remain silent or mess up the shoot, so that is what we did. The publicist was standing next to me, and we both looked up to see the shutters on a façade slowly open with the appropriate creaking noise and then watched as they slowly closed again. My first thought was that being on the back lot they had been rigged to do that; however, looking over at the publicist and seeing his eyes wide, staring at the façade, I knew something wasn't right. The director yelled "cut," and the publicist turned to me and asked, "What the f… was that?"

I said, "You mean it doesn't just do that on its own?"

The publicist told me that the reason he chose this spot for the shoot was because it hadn't been used in years and that the whole thing was nothing but a façade with nothing behind it. I decided to check behind the building, and sure enough, it was empty, just the back side of the façade.

We didn't have time to ponder what we had just seen, because it was time for Butch to drive the replica Munster Koach around the square for the show. They had actually driven the car from Barris's shop close by the studio lot and drove it out to the square so Butch could climb in. Butch was supposed to drive around in a circle until the director yelled "cut." Unfortunately, Butch wouldn't make it that far.

Butch Patrick made it through the first lap, but on the second pass, the rear driver's side wheel came completely off. The tires are known as "wrinkle tires" and are huge. The car was driven over from the shop, driven onto the lot and checked out before being used. To this day, there is no logical explanation for the tire to have come off, nor do I have a logical explanation for the shutters opening and closing other than someone having fun with us.

After finishing the film shoot, Butch asked the driver to stop at sound stage 28. He explained to me that it was known as the "Phantom Stage," because that is where *The Phantom of the Opera* was filmed. He also told me it had a haunted reputation. When we entered the stage, I was immediately greeted by the spirit of an English actor. He was trying to explain to me

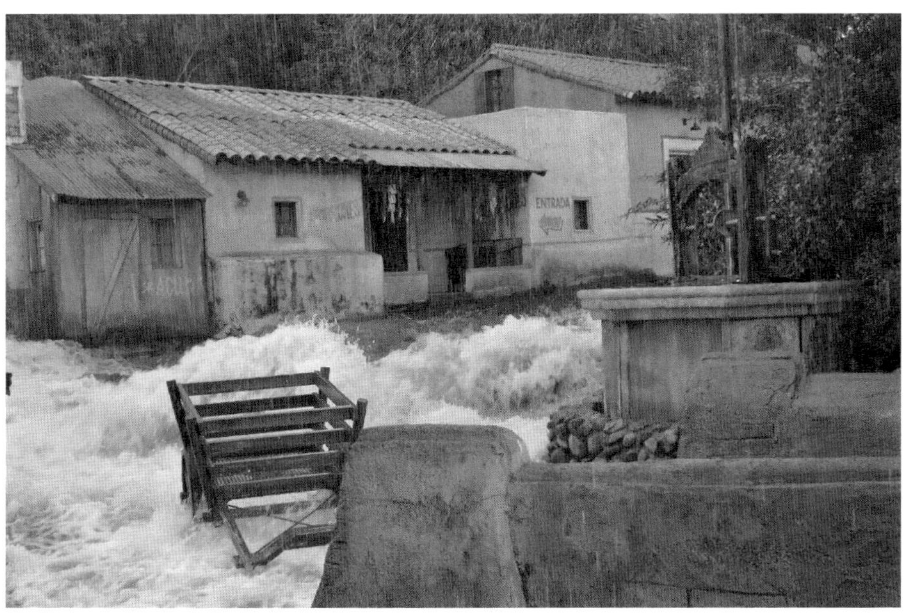

The flash flood special effects still thrill guests more than thirty years after their creation.

what he was doing there. He seemed very upset that talkies had been invented and felt they cost him his career. People do talk about a caped spirit here, but that also was the fashion of the day. I saw no sign of Lon Chaney, however.

We couldn't stay long because the stage was in use, and we didn't want to get in the way. But now that the stage has been torn down and the opera set saved, it will be interesting to see where the spirit person decides to go next.

On another trip back to the studio for an interview for the Hallmark show *Home & Family*, I went back to the Munster House. The whole house now looks very normal, with real grass and plants out front. It was changed for *Desperate Housewives.* But for someone who is a medium and channel, this was a very interesting day. The latent energy of all those films and television shows are soaked into the very fabric of the studio, and paranormal experiences from the back lot of Universal Studios abound.

Bonnie Vent is owner of Genesis Creations Entertainment. She is also a medium/channeler, a paranormal author and vlogger with numerous books and DVDs to her credit. She works with Amazon as a merch designer and is a web developer and content creator.

BIBLIOGRAPHY

Birchard, Robert S. *Early Universal City*. Charleston, SC: Arcadia Publishing, 2009.

Bryant, Kelly. "12 Things That Will Surprise You About Universal Studios Hollywood." Mental Floss. March 13, 2015. http://mentalfloss.com/article/62169/12-things-will-surprise-you-about-universal-studios-hollywood.

Classic-Horror.com. "Reviewing the History of Horror Movies, Universal." http://classic-horror.com/masters/universal.

CreepyLA.com. "The Doomed Aviator Haunting the Universal Studios Backlot." October 7, 2016. http://creepyla.com/2016/10/07/doomed-aviator-haunting-the-universal-studios-backlot-ghost.

Dirks, Tim. "The History of Film, The Pre-1920s." AMC Filmsite. http://www.filmsite.org/pre20sintro3.html.

Earlyaviators.com. "Frank Stites 1882–1915." http://www.earlyaviators.com/estites.htm.

Entertainment Designer. "The History of Universal Studios Hollywood." Last modified November 2, 2011. http://entertainmentdesigner.com/history-of-theme-parks/the-history-of-universal-studios-hollywood.

Funding Universe. "Universal Studios, Inc. History." http://www.fundinguniverse.com/company-histories/universal-studios-inc-history.

Gennawey, Sam. "The Very Early History of Universal Studios Hollywood." Micechat. March 7, 2013. http://micechat.com/23267-universal-studios.

IMDb. "Carl Laemmle." https://m.imdb.com/name/nm0480674/bio.

Klein, Christopher. "The Renegade Roots of Hollywood Studios." A&E. April 30, 2012. https://www.google.com/amp/amp.history.com/news/the-renegade-roots-of-hollywood-studios.

LATourist. "Universal Studios Theme Park." https://www.latourist.com/index.php?page=universal-studios-theme-park.

Murdy, John. "The World Famous Universal Studio Tour." Universal Studios Hollywood. http://www.thestudiotour.com/ush/studiotour/history.php.

Stanca Mustea, Christina. "Carl Laemmle." In *Immigrant Entrepreneurship: German-American Business Biographies*. Vol. 4 *1720 to Present*, edited by Jeffrey Fear. German Historical Institute. Last modified June 19, 2012. https://www.immigrantentrepreneurship.org/entry.php?rec=55.

Taste of Cinema. "The 15 Best Classic Horror Film from Universal Studios." Last modified October 7, 2014. http://www.tasteofcinema.com/2014/the-15-best-classic-horror-films-from-universal-studio.

About the Authors

Brian Clune is the co-founder and the historian for Planet Paranormal Radio and Planet Paranormal Investigations. He has traveled the entire state of California researching its haunted hot spots and historical locations in an effort to bring knowledge of the paranormal and the wonderful history of the state to those interested in learning.

His interest in history has led him to volunteer aboard the USS *Iowa* and the Fort MacArthur Military Museum in addition to lecturing at colleges and universities around the state. He has been involved with numerous TV shows, including *Ghost Adventures*, *My Ghost Story*, *Dead Files* and *Ghost Hunters* and was the subject in a companion documentary for the movie *Paranormal Asylum*.

His other books include *California's Historic Haunts* (Schiffer Books) and the highly acclaimed *Ghosts of the Queen Mary* (The History Press), both with Bob Davis. He is also the author of *Haunted San Pedro* (The History Press) and *Hollywood Obscura* (Schiffer Books), a spellbinding book dealing with Hollywood's dark and sordid tales of murder and ghosts. He is currently working on a book about the haunted history of Alcatraz Prison.

Clune lives in Southern California with his loving wife, Terri, his three wonderful children and, of course, Wandering Wyatt!

Bob Davis is a commercial real estate investor by day and a paranormal researcher by night. Bob co-owns Planet Paranormal Radio, Planet Paranormal Investigations and Queen Mary Shadows along with Ash

Blackwell and Brian Clune. Bob lives in Southern California with his lovely wife, Miyu, and son Nick. His daughter Katrina, also a paranormal researcher, is currently living and investigating in Arizona, where Planet Paranormal investigators enjoy investigating new locations.

Davis has been on over thirty-five radio broadcasts nationally and internationally and has been featured in ten books and publications and two documentary films.

In addition, he has been published in the *New York Daily News*, *World News*, the *LA Examiner* and the *Paranormal Examiner* and has been seen on such hit television shows as *Ghost Hunters*, *Ghost Adventures*, *My Ghost Story and The Dead Files.*

The authors' book Ghosts of the Queen Mary *was featured in the October 2015 edition of* Life *magazine's World's Most Haunted Places edition as the subject for the Queen Mary segment.*

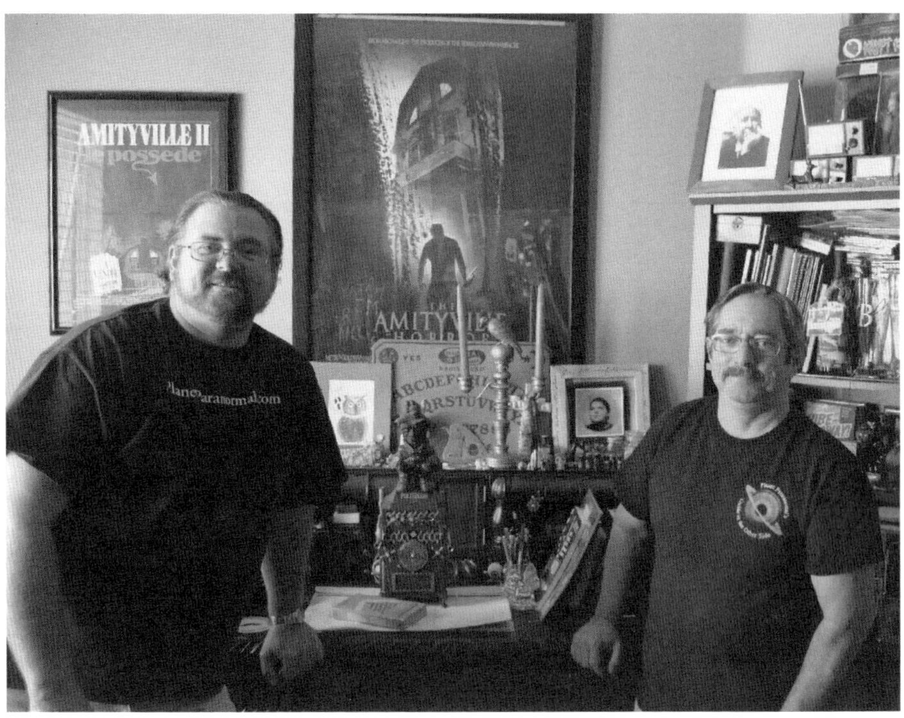

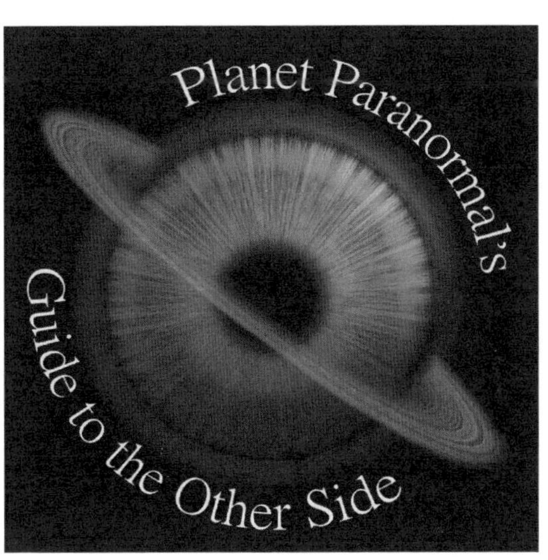
Planet Paranormal's
Guide to the Other Side